INTERCULTURAL
COMMUNICATION IN ACTION

Borgo Press Books by FRANCIS JARMAN

Culture and Identity (editor)
Encountering the Other (editor)
The Gate of Lemnos: A Science Fiction Novel
Girls Will Be Girls: A Play
Intercultural Communication in Action (editor)
Invictus: A Play
Lip Service: A Play
A Star Fell: A Play
*White Skin, Dark Skin, Power, Dream: Collected Essays on
    Literature & Culture*

INTERCULTURAL COMMUNICATION IN ACTION

FRANCIS JARMAN, EDITOR

THE BORGO PRESS

MMXII

Borgo Perspectives on Intercultural Communication
Number Two

INTERCULTURAL COMMUNICATION IN ACTION

FIRST EDITION

Published by Wildside Press LLC

www.wildsidebooks.com

DEDICATION

For WOLFGANG LÖFFLER (1944-2010)

CONTENTS

INTRODUCTION
INTERCULTURAL COMMUNICATION

INTERCULTURAL COMMUNICATION IS a new and highly eclectic discipline, so new, in fact, that, when he was asked, the head of a university library that I know was most unwilling to organize an area of book stacks for such a wildly interdisciplinary subject (although he had had no problems doing so in the similar case of Gender Studies). The books, he argued, should remain in the subject areas where they were—and he was indeed saving his staff a lot of work, because if you took the time to make a list of those subjects, it would give you a strong idea of just how eclectic intercultural communication really is. You would have books from anthropology, business and management studies, education, history, international relations, linguistics, organization studies, philosophy, political science, psychology, religious studies, social work, and sociology, with a few from art and literature as well (and I may well have missed something).

Nor is it easy to say who started or "founded" it. To some extent, like Topsy in Harriet Beecher Stowe's novel *Uncle Tom's Cabin*, it "never was born", but just "grow'd" (263 f.). Two names do stand out, however, as internationally popular figures (and this much to the chagrin of some serious-minded academic specialists): the American anthropologist *Edward T. Hall* (1914-2009), and the Dutchman *Geert Hofstede* (b. 1928). Hall, who wrote both copiously and attractively, popularized such concepts as "high or low context", "proxemics" and "chronemics", and helped to give a jolt to the complacent social science mindset of "Sociology does the West, anthropology does the rest". Leaving aside his scholarly achievements, Hofstede would have earned his place in any intercultural hall of fame if only by virtue of the fact that he attracted the interest of big business to intercultural communication, opening up unprecedented funding possibilities for intercultural research; his *Cultures and Organizations: Software of the Mind* became the bible of intercultural wisdom for managers and businessmen worldwide. Intercultural communication would now be taken seriously by people who had money and power.

Go further back in time, though, and you will find such major figures as the Greek historian *Herodotus* (fifth century BC), not only the "Father of History"—a well-known cliché— but the "Father" of "culturally aware travel", too, and perhaps the very first human being to travel widely out of curiosity and for personal intellectual pleasure. Or the French essayist *Michel de Montaigne* (1533-92), the "first modern man" and the first great cultural and ethical relativist (incidentally, an inspiration for Shakespeare's troubled thinker Hamlet, who declares that "there is nothing either good or bad but thinking makes it so", *Hamlet*, II, 2, ll. 249 f.). Writing about the newly-discovered "cannibals" of the Caribbean islands, Montaigne declared:

> I find (from what has been told me) that there is nothing savage or barbarous about those peoples, but that every man calls barbarous anything he is not accustomed to; it is indeed the case that we have no other criterion of truth or right-reason than the example and form of the opinions and customs of our own country. There we always find the perfect religion, the perfect polity, the most developed and perfect way of doing anything! ("On the Cannibals", 7 f.)

Wherever it might come from, and whatever it might be (or, rather, however it may best be approached, *i.e.*, described and analyzed), intercultural communication is now an important aspect of life in most parts of the world. It is essential that we get it right, for a number of reasons.

Firstly, because if we don't it may cost us a lot of money (and this is why the world of business has taken to the subject so enthusiastically, if at times naïvely) or cost us more than just cash (when intercultural misunderstandings lead to hatred, violence and war).

Secondly, because the more that we get it it wrong, the more likely it becomes—through the workings of a vicious circle on one or even both sides of the interactional divide—that intercultural communication will become even more difficult in future.

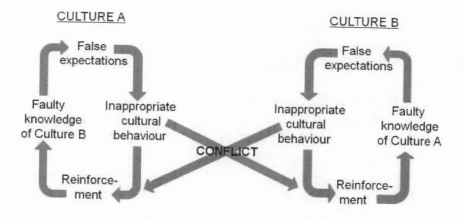

The Vicious Circles of Misunderstanding (Jarman 2003)

And, thirdly, because of the huge opportunities for learning and synergistic action that become available to us through an intelligent and open-minded interaction—a *dialog*—with the Other. The greatest unused resources that we can draw upon are not in the Amazon jungles, or the oceans, or even in outer space, but in the thoughts, ideas, skills, styles and solutions of other human beings.

Even in an increasingly globalized and networked world it will be an uphill struggle, since greater *exposure* to alien thoughts and values is in itself no guarantee that these will be understood. The students in the photo on the cover may well be studying American Literature, but they have probably only very restricted knowledge of the culture that produced it, and next to no understanding of the values that resonate in the texts that they are reading (indeed, in the case of Middle Eastern students like these, the more that they actually discover about those values, the more likely it is that they will reject them with scorn and indignation).

The following essays will therefore look at different aspects of intercultural communication in action, "as it happens", or in the various ways that we may try to help it along.

THIS IS THE second book in a series with the broader title *Borgo Perspectives on Intercultural Communication*. The essays are—as the title of the volume suggests—about the practical side of intercultural communication, and venture into such areas as the **internet**, the **media**, **journalism**, **education**, and **language**. The book is dedicated to the memory of my former colleague Professor Dr. Wolfgang Löffler (1944-2010): musician, conductor and composer, scientist, teacher, scholar, linguist, and traveler—above all, a kind, generous and intellectually curious human being.

Most of the contributors are colleagues, former colleagues, former students or friends of mine (these are overlapping categories) from the University of Hildesheim in Germany, but there are also contributions from further afield. The authors come from Britain, Bulgaria, Germany, India, Russia and Spain.

Among the topics, there are essays on student exchanges (BREEDE; DA SILVA) and intercultural training (KUSCHEL, BOSSE & GRIGORIEVA), on biographical research as an intercultural approach (DRAWERT), and on intercultural aspects of the internet (GRIESBAUM; MANDL; MÖSTL, WOMSER-HACKER & GRIESBAUM). There are contributions which look at intercultural film analysis (JARMAN), television shows (LANGNER) and journalism (RAMANAN; METZ & DANOVA), language and immigrant groups (BAIGORRI & OTERO; JARMAN), the revealing differences in the way that the English and the Germans construct meaning (BITTNER), language learning as a joyful experience both for young children and for their teachers (SOFRONIEVA), and language as a means to reduce rather than exacerbate Otherness (SCHUBERT).

The listings of "References" at the end of some of the contributions are precisely that—listings of works directly referred to or quoted from—and are not intended to be full academic bibliographies. Where online sources are given, the date of most recent access is (unless otherwise indicated) January 20th, 2011.

The views expressed in these essays are not necessarily those of the editor, the publisher or of fellow contributors.

THE FIRST VOLUME in this series, *Encountering the Other*, offered a selection of widely differing personal descriptions of encounters with cultural Otherness; and essays about intercultural aspects of politeness, everyday contact, seduction, and war. The third volume will be about *Culture and Identity*.

The series has two "homes". The first is the Institute of Intercultural Communication at Hildesheim University, Germany, which is where I happen to teach and research.

I would like to thank my Hildesheim colleague Annette Graën for her help with the manuscript; Brit Bohot-Behnke for the cover photo; those students or former students whose film analyses I have drawn upon for examples in my account of the Hildesheim Intercultural Film Database: Ilia Barancic, Inga Bartelt, Eva Bergold, Katrin Bonkat, Dorthe Dalgaard Jensen, Anke Dettmar, Vy Do, Lea Drolshagen, Ann Eckert, Benedikta Grissemann, Raéla Hagemann, Johanna Hoefer, Roland Kemmer, Iris Kohler, Berenike Kuschel, Dominika Lukoszek, Simone Praulich, Felicitas Quass, Jana Schilling, Anne Schulz, Claudia Schumacher, André Schwentuchowski, Birte Sechtig, Ina Siebald, Melize da Silva Colucci, Nina Wiessner, Ariane

Wilhus and Ewa Zatońska; and Björn Quast, who set up the database for me and still manages it technically.

The series is also at home at Wildside's Borgo Press, where I should like to thank my editor, Professor Michael Burgess, for his encouragement, support, and unfailing patience.

—FRANCIS JARMAN
Hildesheim, Germany
January 2011

References

Hofstede, Geert / Hofstede, Gert Jan. *Cultures and Organizations: Software of the Mind* (1991). Second edition. New York: McGraw-Hill, 2005.

Jarman, Francis. "Fremdwahrnehmung und interkulturelle Kommunikation: Kreatives Potenzial ensteht aus der Kultur der Verschiedenartigkeit." In: *BRANDaktuell*, 3, 2003, 24 f.; 4, 2003, 25.

Montaigne, Michel de. "On the Cannibals." In: *Four Essays*. Transl. M. A. Screech. Harmondsworth, Middx.: Penguin, 1995, 1-26.

Shakespeare, William. *Hamlet*. Ed. Harold Jenkins. The Arden Edition of the Works of William Shakespeare. London / New York: Routledge, 1989.

Stowe, Harriet Beecher. *Uncle Tom's Cabin: A Tale of Life among the Lowly*. London: George Routledge & Co., 1852.

STUDYING ABROAD TO ENCOUNTER THE OTHER?

by MARIT BREEDE

ALMOST 290 APPLICATIONS—that's a new record for the University of Hildesheim. About 290 students are going to spend the winter semester 2010-11 abroad. They've understood that going abroad for some time—and that means more than just a couple of days in Paris or two weeks in Mallorca—is a must if you want to have a good chance on the job market.

Despite obstacles like the hunt for credit points and the lack of time due to a stricter study program, students are—at least at the University of Hildesheim—becoming more mobile. And the trend is that Europe is not enough. There are more and more students coming to my office hours (I work at the International Office of the university), asking for advice on how to get to the USA, Canada, Australia, New Zealand, Africa or Asia. Europe? How boring! You can do that in weekend trips. And besides, we Europeans are so similar—that's not really *abroad*, is it?

So, every year a large number of students go abroad to study or to do an internship in another country. But why? What are their reasons for doing this, other than to further their own career?

Of course there is no single answer that is valid for everybody. In general, it's a mixture of reasons, and every student has his or her own focus. But some reasons for going abroad seem to apply in almost all cases, the most common ones being:

because you *have* to, that is, the curriculum requires a semester abroad; because you want or have to improve your language skills; because you want to improve your chances of getting a good job; because nearly all your friends are going (that doesn't apply to every degree course); because you want to have a time-out from the daily grind of your boring and stressful studies; or because you're looking for new ideas and perspectives. All in all, I have the impression that "encountering the Other" is *not* the main objective of most of the students who go abroad. It's perhaps only one of a number of reasons and I believe, for most of them, not the main one.

An indicator of this is one of the remarks that we hear most often at the International Office: "Well, you know, I study XYZ and so I *have* to go abroad for one semester..." The first time I heard this, I couldn't stop myself asking: "Oh, so you don't actually *want* to?" Now I know better, and I bite my tongue. For this type of student, it's clearly the curriculum which is the main reason for them going abroad, and they'll try to get the bothersome business over with as quickly as they can. They prefer to "go out" (*i.e.*, abroad) for as short a time as possible, they expect you to organize everything for them, and they are appalled to hear that there is information that they'll have to track down for themselves (on how to get there, which courses to take, and so on). Sometimes they—especially the girls—are very determined not to go alone, but only with their best friend. In short, what they are looking for is a way of doing it that seems to be both safe and comfortable.

Naturally there is also the other type, the adventurer or explorer. Students come to us and tell us (for instance) about their plans to go to South Africa, to work there in a school and to travel afterwards. For them, it's mainly the new perspectives and the challenge of the unknown which lure them. I love talking to these students because they are so committed, so *looking forward* to the big adventure, and you become part of this by giving them advice. The greatest reward of all is to read later in an email: "Thanks for helping me with my plans. It was the best time I've ever had!"

THOSE STUDENTS WHO skip programs like ERASMUS [the student mobility program of the European Union—*Ed.*], where most steps are regulated and you follow a certain routine, are in general highly organized. In spite of the fact that they more or less have to organize everything on their own, they tend to have fewer problems with obstacles like finance, finding accommodation, making the travel arrangements, *etc.* Of course you will also find the well-organized type of student among the ERASMUS outgoings ["outgoings" are students who leave their own university to go abroad; those who come from abroad, in a parallel movement more or less filling the places that the former have left, are known as "incomings"—*Ed.*]. Other outgoing students are less sure of themselves, and some of them will drop in every couple of days to ask about the next step that they have to undertake and to make sure that they haven't forgotten anything. Others don't care at all and get in a flap and become nervous as the date of departure draws closer and they realize that they aren't prepared at all.

The obstacles you have to overcome if you want to study abroad are the same for nearly everyone: making sure you have enough money, finding accommodation, battling with all those regulations within the ERASMUS program and/or at the university abroad, choosing the right courses with the right number of credit points, coping with a sometimes very different way of studying, struggling with a foreign language and—most of all—with other habits. For me, the worst day was around the third or the fourth—I was getting tired, my language ability seemed to be getting *worse* rather than better, I was fed up with the noisy people around me and their stupid behavior—and I felt lonely. Today, the majority of universities have a good tutoring system, with student "buddies", international offices and groups like ERASMUS on Tour which organize social activities and excursions for exchange students. Besides, almost everywhere you have good internet access, and Skype or chat programs give you a reliable link to your friends and family at home.

But even so, the beginning of a semester abroad isn't all that easy and sometimes it can be really tough. In some cases, it's just *too* tough and the student decides to give up and to come home. The trigger may sometimes be something that could hardly have been anticipated—an unfriendly facility manager, dirty accommodation with moldy rooms, unsuitable courses at the partner university—and the reaction of the student may be disproportionate, but in nearly all cases whatever it was that happened proved to be simply "the final straw". The general feeling of the student is that he or she can't cope with this new situation, and that everything is just too much to handle. Every year, we have one to three such cases of students packing their bags and coming home, mainly because of psychological problems. And of course we ask ourselves then what the real problem was, and whether we could have done anything to prevent it happening. But this question of just how far you can go in shepherding your students is one that is too vast and complicated to be dealt with here.

FORTUNATELY, IN MOST cases the students get over their first shock and learn to cope with their new situation. And they actually begin to enjoy their semester abroad. They enjoy being with other exchange students, going to ERASMUS parties, getting to know a new system in a new environment with new people, and making new friends.

And this brings us to our point, since of course the students *do* "encounter the Other" during their exchange semester. At most partner universities you are not the only exchange student, but meet students from quite a number of other countries, so you are part of an international group and your chances to having some interesting intercultural experiences are not insubstantial.

Allow me a short comment here. In my opinion, it's important to be aware that this encounter isn't the same as *immersing yourself* in the daily life of the country that you're now studying in. The group of ERASMUS students (we often call it an ERASMUS-

Rudel in German, that is, a "pack" of Erasmus students) is—to employ a familiar metaphor—like a bubble within a bubble. This international group has its own culture and habits, and the university around it also has its own academic culture, so you shouldn't mistake this for the daily life of "normal" Spaniards or French people or whatever. If you truly want to get to know their way of life, then it is better to choose an internship or to work as a volunteer in Africa, where you may be the only foreigner amongst the locals, and be forced to speak their language rather than the *lingua franca* English. So the immersion in the host country's daily life tends not to be very deep in the case of most of the Erasmus or other exchange students. Nevertheless, they have the opportunity to encounter different nationalities and deal with different cultures.

Besides, as I noted above, for most of the students "encountering the Other" was hardly their main objective, and even if some of them do write in their reports that they would have liked to get to know more of the local people, cultural immersion was not the principal reason why they went abroad.

One thing seems very well worth pointing out, and it is something that is the same for everybody, both for exchange students and for trainees, for outgoings who are in touch with the locals as well as for those who prefer to stay in the "pack" of other Erasmus students: they come to realize how *German* they are. Sometimes they tell us later: "It's so much more relaxed there, so much better than here in Germany." Sometimes they get irritated over the different attitude to (let's say) punctuality. For some of them, it's hard to get used to the fact that their Spanish friends will inevitably turn up half an hour late. One of our students told me that she appreciated the German approach to studying much more after her stay in France because, even after the Bologna reforms to higher education, you still had more freedom to choose your courses and the courses were more participative and you were not just sitting there listening and writing down whatever the lecturer at the front was talking about.

So, during their stay abroad, the students learn something about their own culture. And they get better at coping with new situations, they get tougher, and more self-confident. During a conference last week, a colleague who works in the international office of another university, also in the outgoings section, put it this way: "When they come back, some of them have changed a lot. They talk differently, they behave in a different way, and you can feel how much their confidence has grown after they have spent a semester or a year abroad."

The stay abroad shapes you; it is an intense experience that you won't quickly forget. After all, you've overcome obstacles, you've coped with a weird environment and with strange people, and you're now aware that you are reasonably well prepared for some of the other challenges that life may throw at you.

On Facebook and other social networking sites you will find an astonishing number of groups catering for people suffering from what might be called the "ERASMUS blues", dreaming of the time when they were free of the daily burdens at their home university, free from stressful and boring studies, and instead successfully fighting their way through the jungle of a foreign country. This reaction can be so strong that quite a lot of the outgoing students go abroad again and again—as trainees, volunteers, travelers... there are so many possibilities.

When the outgoing students come back to our university, they are often still feeling the thrill of their experience. They may also be feeling the shock of returning to their grey daily life, though that will pass. The enthusiasm will of course pass, too. But it is frequently so strong that the former outgoing students are eager to share it with others. One possible platform for this is the meeting between former outgoings and younger students who are interested in going abroad that we organize once a semester. Here, students who've come back can talk about the partner universities that they went to, and they often do it so animatedly, with pictures and funny stories, that you would just love to set off at once and go there yourself. That is the best publicity for student mobility that you can imagine! Some of them go even further and volunteer to act as "buddies" to the incoming students expected at our university, supporting in this practical way the cause of internationalization at home.

You often observe how the majority of the outgoing students feel a bond with the foreign university that they went to, and with that particular country, for a long, long time. For me personally, it has been nearly ten years now, but my heart still beats faster when I get an email from our partner university in Castellón in Spain, where I spent my own ERASMUS semester—even if it is a dry official message relating to routine administrative stuff from colleagues at the International Office! And it is interesting that students who go to more "exotic" countries like Latvia or Portugal, countries for which they may not have been prepared by several semesters of courses in the relevant language or by appropriate cultural studies seminars, seem to develop the deepest bond. One reason for this could be that they are outside the "mainstream" of student mobility, to countries like Britain, France and Spain, so the challenge—but also the reward—is greater for them.

Nearly all the students declare their satisfaction with their semester abroad in their final report. Though they may criticize certain aspects of the administrative organization, of the partner university, or other subjects, the final grade that they give in their evaluation is in more than ninety per cent of cases four or five points out of five. So it seems that they don't regret having gone abroad!

To RETURN TO the question: What role does the "encounter with the Other" play for students who spend a semester abroad? I would say that at first sight, and explicitly, it doesn't seem to be an important factor. After all, you seldom hear a student say that he or she wants to go abroad "to encounter the Other". But behind the manifest reasons given and in the actual experiences that the students have, the influence of the daily encounter with the Other is indeed important. Even in the ERASMUS bubble! How intense this encounter has been and to what extent the students were able to get a glimpse of the daily life of the locals, of their thoughts and habits, varies from student to student and depends not only on their personality but also on the environment and the setting—for example, whether it was an internship or part of an ERASMUS exchange. The same is true with regard to the other expectations that the students may have expressed before they went abroad: there's no guarantee that they will have improved their language skills, especially if they spent most of their time in the company of their best friend or with a group of other Germans, and, since nowadays nearly everybody has spent some time abroad, you can't say that it is guaranteed to give them a substantial advantage on the job market. What you *can* say, though, is that they'll have gained some new perspectives.

What is almost certain, however, is that the students will have changed. By encountering the Other and struggling with unfamiliar behavior and situations, they will have encountered *themselves* during that time abroad. Because, much like what happens when you look into a mirror, the encounter with the Other is an encounter with yourself. And the more intense that encounter with other cultures, other ways of thinking and behaving, proves to be, the better you will get to know yourself, and your own way of thinking, acting and reacting.

I can't imagine many of the students brooding over such matters while they are filling in their application forms for ERASMUS, nor will they necessarily think much about them after they have come back, but the experience of studying abroad will nevertheless shape their lives—in a positive way.

QUALITATIVE APPROACHES TO STUDENTS' INTERCULTURAL EXPERIENCE

by VASCO DA SILVA

THE NEED FOR intercultural knowledge in a globalized world is an obvious one. Students, seeking work after their education, now have to have international skills which are not limited simply to knowing one or two foreign languages. Their *curriculum vitae* must include at least one stay abroad, showing their ability to cope with a different culture, to live under other everyday conditions, to acquire experience and to learn from it.

In 1987, the then European Community (which became the European Union in 1992) recognized that need, and started the funding program ERASMUS, an acronym for "European Community Action Scheme for the Mobility of University Students". Nowadays, ERASMUS is a synonym for student mobility in Europe, with more than 100,000 students traveling throughout the continent each year. The idea is quite simple: universities from thirty-two different countries (all the European Union member states plus Iceland, Norway, Switzerland, Liechtenstein and Turkey, and in the near future Croatia) cooperate with each other, mainly in the field of student teacher mobility. Thus, students are allowed to study for up to one year abroad, and academic staff can teach a certain number of hours at a foreign university.

Despite the huge success of this program (DAAD 2008, 25), there has been a noticeable lack of qualitative research in this area. Most of the studies of ERASMUS deal with quantitative data, thereby offering suggestions to nation states as to how they can increase their number of outgoing students. National mobility agencies like the German DAAD (*Deutscher Akademischer Austauschdienst*, German Academic Exchange Service) publish so-called "Success Stories" (*e.g.*, DAAD 2007) about former exchange students returning home and reporting on their experiences to a wider audience. As their one and only purpose is to highlight the *advantages* of such a stay abroad, they tend not to cover difficult situations or even failed experiences in dealing with other cultures. The following essay suggests that researchers should focus more on the subjective view of these stays abroad to find out how students make sense of their (intercultural) experience, how they manage to "survive" such a stay abroad, and with what experiences—both positive and negative—they return. Three different approaches will be examined and the initial findings presented.

Accompanying Students during Their Stay Abroad

ACCESSING THE STUDENTS' experience can be done, basically, in two ways. On the one hand, researchers can ask returners to tell their story orally or in writing. On the other hand, the students can be "accompanied" step by step during their stay abroad.

The latter approach is currently being followed by at least two research projects in Germany. Although they are focused more or less on the same topics and are based on the same theory, they started off as individual projects and "found each other" at two conferences on intercultural learning and training in 2009. Both the "PIKK" project (German acronym for *Portfolio Interkulturelle Kommunikation und Kompetenz*, portfolio on intercultural communication and competence), being carried out at Hildesheim University, and the "Portico" project, at the University of Applied Sciences in Zwickau, use the so-called portfolio method and have set out to achieve the same goals: to help students get a deeper insight into their host culture and be better able to reflect on critical situations or even problems. Researchers take a closer look at what students are doing during their stay abroad, how they manage and how they react to certain problems or difficulties. The procedure is quite simple. Students are given a questionnaire and/or particular tasks at fixed moments during their stay abroad. They are asked to answer the questions or fulfill the tasks by a certain date. They then upload their results onto an online platform hosted by Hildesheim University, which also functions as a social web space ("CollabUni", see GRIESBAUM in this volume). As this website is a closed one, to which only chosen members have access (for instance students and staff of Hildesheim University and their invited guests), the entries by the students are secure and not publicly accessible. Alternatively, they have the opportunity to post their answers directly to the staff members on the portfolio team, so that they are the only people who will read them. In this way, the more sensitive material (such as is likely to be generated, for example, when students become aware of problems that affect them closely as individuals, and don't want their answers to be read and discussed openly on the internet) is safe.

What kinds of tasks or questions are the students set? At Hildesheim University, they receive these tasks at four fixed points, and as their average stay abroad is six months, usually during the winter semester, the tasks are sent out approximately every couple of months. The first block of questions is online after the first two months of their stay, the second shortly before Christmas, the third is made accessible just before they start packing their suitcases, and the final block is sent out after their return to Germany. In the beginning, the sojourners tend to learn about intercultural competence in general, as this portfolio is also aimed at students who have not had any previous intercultural training. In this first round, students are asked to reflect upon the state of their knowledge, with special focus on their personal contacts and language learning level. The aim is to prepare the ground for further reflection later on. The second block mainly focuses on linguistic aspects of intercultural communication. The students receive theoretical input in the form of short texts made available through the online platform mentioned earlier. Here, they need to pay attention to everyday phenomena like nonverbal communication or indexical expressions of the foreign language that they are using on a daily basis—"indexicals" are expressions whose meaning changes with the context in which they are used. This language may be the national language of the host country or a *lingua franca* English, as used, among others, for instance in Norway, Turkey or many countries in Asia. Shortly before they return, the focus of the tasks reverts to round one. The students are now requested to compare their initial statements (regarding their personal contacts, cultural and semantic observations or experience in dealing with cultural differences) with the observations and perceptions they have made during their whole stay abroad up to this point near the end of their sojourn. They are always asked to do this in a reflexive manner. Dealing with your own thoughts and observations and comparing these to the current state of your knowledge can lead potentially to an awareness of how your own intercultural and/or linguistic competence has evolved. After their return to Germany, the students summarize their entire stay abroad, and reflect upon the intercultural experiences that they had during this time. They are asked to describe critical incidents (a method which can also be used in another way, as will be explained below) and to evaluate the development of their own intercultural competence. As this last round of tasks takes place a certain time *after* their return, some cognitive processes may already have been going on. Thus a more critical reflection can be expected than what they formulate shortly before they return to their home country.

This way, students see how they gain intercultural competence in a reflexive way. Accompanying sojourners helps them to use the rich experience that they have abroad and turn it into cognitive and behavioral competence. Furthermore, students could deal with their problems and perceived difficulties more effectively through this journal-like approach. With theoretical inputs on hand, they could find solutions to problems on their own, or at least perceive the problems not so much as negative aspects of a stay abroad than as challenges that arise in intercultural encounters. As students upload their answers and postings onto a private portfolio space throughout the entire stay, they acquire a rich and varied collection of material about their time abroad. Blogging and sharing photos are common and widely-used ways to report on your time abroad. With the "CollabUni" platform, they have free space for staying in contact with their friends and families at home. Students can choose to do both, using the portfolio *and* these tools. As these projects are still only in their second year, concrete empirical analysis still has to be done, however, to verify the outcomes and the use of the tools described above.

Yet there are findings which can already be presented even after just one year of using this method: Self-assessments by the students suggest that a portfolio during a stay abroad makes it easier for them to tackle their challenges. The permanent contact to the home university provides them with a feeling of not being left alone in the host country. One student in the 2009-10 sample put it like this:

> The portfolio led me in a well-directed way to pay attention to cultural differences and to reflect upon them critically but not judgementally.
> Unlike my last stay in that host country, this time I became more aware of the things I was doing. The portfolio supported me in getting to the core of the culture and showed me in which areas I still need to work on my skills (my translation).

Not only that, the researchers obtain rich documentation of happenings in the host culture, of the different ways of thinking about and dealing with difficulties, and—in the long run—of the student's development of "accompanied intercultural competence". The huge amount of qualitative data created by the participants is ripe for examination, as this subjective material potentially offers deep insights into personal coping strategies through the eyes of the participants during their stay abroad.

Using Retrospective Storytelling Afterwards

ANOTHER WAY OF gaining qualitative data is to ask returners to tell their story about their stay abroad. This can be done in very different ways. I want to highlight two studies, one research project already completed and one currently in progress.

There is a long tradition of using critical incidents as an approach to problem perception and coping strategies. Flanagan started to use reported critical incidents back in 1954 to train US Air Force pilots for emergency situations. The critical incident technique (CIT) was introduced in intercultural communication by Fiedler *et al.* in 1971. Flanagan himself stated that the CIT "consists of a set of procedures for collecting direct observations of human behavior in such a way as to facilitate their potential usefulness in solving practical problems" (327). By recounting critical situations, students connect the core problem with context information, which again is crucial information for the researchers. In this way, not only problems and problematic situations themselves can be investigated, but more especially how the students *felt* during that situation and how they managed to deal with it. The resulting subjective view of the situation is not a disadvantage; in fact, it is a goal of that method "to gain an understanding of the incident from the perspective of the individual, taking into account cognitive, affective and behavioral elements" (Chell 1998, 56).

In 2008, the critical incident technique was applied in Zwickau. Students returning from a recently finished stay abroad in Spain or France were asked to write an account of two critical incidents that they had experienced during that year. As they were students of applied linguistics with an obligatory year abroad, they received intense intercultural training before and after their sojourn. Back in Germany, they had to describe two critical incidents, analyze them by themselves and give retrospective possible solutions. This material was then subjected to careful scrutiny (da Silva 2010).

When used as an intercultural training tool in a post-sojourn period, the critical incident technique revealed three stages of self-reflexivity (da Silva, 71 f.). To describe the incident and discern a problem, students have to have skills relevant to observation and recognition. In this stage, students in a first step trace the problems back Mostly to those persons involved in the trouble, which Krewer (1994) describes as "ethnocentric personalization" (149). Although they relate the problems directly to the persons, they seek the *reasons* for that behavior not in personal but in general cultural factors. Therefore, in their reporting of critical incidents mentioned above, a huge number of the students used cultural generalizations ("typical German" or "as is typically done in Spain") to describe why the problems occurred, despite the fact that they might also have been caused by interpersonal conflicts. This "culturalistic overinterpretation" (Krewer) is a first step towards understanding the incident, provided that a deeper analysis follows. This first stage is crucial for a solution of the critical incident—by recognizing the problem and being able to describe it, students prepare themselves for a possible modification of behavior. But note: these processes might not happen during the critical incident itself, but retrospectively. Therefore the description and self-analysis may prepare the ground for a possible modification of behavior in the future.

When students are asked to analyze the reported critical incidents, they consider the context and—for the most part—add the perspective of their interlocutor to their point of view. Furthermore, they use theories of intercultural communication to get a more "external" perspective on the situation. In doing this, they put themselves into a *metaposition*, which can be seen as the second of the three stages of self reflexivity. The interpretation of the situation through their own *and* the eyes of their communication partners amounts to far more than just describing the incident. Or—as Krewer puts it—students reach a "re-personalization" which takes the culture strongly into consideration. Now, they associate the situation with the persons involved, but connect the actions with the culture. In this way, an interactionist, *i.e.*, more subjective, view of the critical incident is created.

After describing and analyzing the incident, students should be able to evolve practical action plans for future situations of the same kind. To do so, they—again—have to take into consideration both their own view of the situation and the view of their interlocutors, so that an "(inter)cultural creativity or synergy" (Krewer) can arise. In the ideal case, the students create a new common culture based upon the two cultures as perceived and analyzed.

In conclusion, the critical incident technique gives researchers not only qualitative data but also a strong instrument for evaluating the outcomes of such a stay abroad with respect to intercultural learning. Both of these—the content of the incidents reported and the ways of describing and analyzing them—help to close the gap that is still evident when it comes to qualitative research on students' stays abroad.

FINALLY, I WOULD like to introduce my own current research project, in which I ask former ERASMUS students to tell the story of their year abroad. In particular, I am interested in German students who went to Spain and entered into a relationship with a Spaniard, and *vice versa*, Spanish students who went to Germany and had a relationship with a German during their stay. This phenomenon is known as "ERASMUS Love"! Despite the fact that its existence is well-known from student reports and articles in non-scholarly journals, it has never (to the best of my knowledge) been given systematic attention. I use auto-biographical narrative interviews (see DRAWERT in this volume), as this method promises the deepest insights into such a partly "taboo" topic. In addition, I reconstruct how the interviewees talk about their stay abroad and about ERASMUS as a political program *and* a way of life at the same time. The European Union's favorite mobility program is far more than just a political way to get students to study at another university. After twenty years of existence, it is also a kind of way of life: You "do ERASMUS", when you go abroad; the "ERASMUS people" is a common way of referring to exchange students; there are special "ERASMUS parties" and "ERASMUS shared flats". As these few (of many possible) examples show, ERASMUS has become a synonym for mobility in higher education in Europe and the many things which accompany such a stay abroad.

This could be very useful for research. In talking about their entire stay and (in this particular project) their love relationship with a member of the host culture, the former exchange students are obliged to reveal often very detailed context information about important phases of their sojourn. Although my own research is more focused on the linguistic act of producing these narratives, researchers who are interested in obtaining qualitative data about students' stays abroad could use the same technique, too. By asking returned students to tell the story of their time abroad, researchers acquire first-hand information about how things work during such a stay, how the interviewees see *their* time abroad and what actually goes on while they are in a foreign country. Although student exchange programs have existed for a long time (structured mobility programs in the European Union, as mentioned, for more than twenty years now), these facts are still a kind of "black box" of the unknown in scholarship. With autobiographical narrative interviews, researchers are able to close that gap in many ways. And, as Halualani (2008, 13) has pointed out, with qualitative interviews researchers can focus on what is going on from the viewpoint of the sojourners—something which has been been widely neglected up to now.

Conclusion

AS WE HAVE seen, there is still a huge gap when it comes to qualitative data about students' sojourns, especially in Europe. Statistical knowledge about how many students "do" ERASMUS every year, what majors they are studying, how much money they need, and so on, has been comprehensively covered. How they manage to *do* ERASMUS, though, how they get to know other people, what impact such a stay abroad has on them, *etc.*—this, as we have seen, has only been investigated in fairly small projects.

Qualitative research, as my own and other articles in this volume show, can be done in many different ways. International student exchanges are a rich topic for research—especially in connection with intercultural communication. As the projects mentioned above reveal, students gain in competence in handling international and intercultural encounters. These data could lead to a better understanding of how this competence actually grows. Qualitative data are rich in subjective viewpoints, individual opinions and small close-ups of the way of life of sojourners. Yet they contain a huge amount of information and, investigated properly, could show how ERASMUS on the individual level is been carried out—socially and linguistically. If Europe and the European Union are to succeed, if they are to be not just an economic area but a living space for more than 300 million deeply interconnected people, more attention must be paid to qualitative research projects focused on individuals— if only to understand how the future European decision-makers perceive and feel about Europe. The same goes for universities throughout the continent: an "international" campus is not created simply by sending out and receiving students within Europe and beyond. Projects to accompany these exchanges, tapping into the rich vein of experience that students acquire during their stays abroad and highlighting the problems and challenges that foreign universities can present, are the best foundation for a sustainable strategy of internationalization and a guarantee of there being new incomings and outgoings for many years to come.

References

Chell, Elizabeth. "Critical Incident Technique." In: *Qualitative Methods and Analysis in Organizational Research: A Practical Guide.* Ed. Gillian Symon / Catherine Cassell. London: Sage, 1998, 51-72.

Deutscher Akademischer Austauschdienst. *Aussergewöhnliche Geschichten und Erlebnisse ehemaliger ERASMUS-Studierender: Success Stories V.* Updated version. Bonn: Deutscher Akademischer Austauschdienst (DAAD), 2007. Website, <http://eu.daad.de/imperia/md/content/eu/74939_daad_succes_stories_5te_gesamt.pdf>

------------. *SOKRATES / ERASMUS 2006 / 2007: Statistische Übersichten zur Studierenden- und Dozentenmobilität.* Bonn: DAAD, 2008.

Fiedler, Fred. E. / Mitchell, Terence / Triandis, Harry C. "The Culture Assimilator: An Approach to Cross-cultural Training." In: *Journal of Applied Psychology,* 1971, 55, 2, 95–102.

Flanagan, John C. "The Critical Incident Technique." In: *Psychological Bulletin,* 1954, 51, 4, 327-59.

Halualani, Rona Tamiko. "How Do Multicultural University Students Define and Make Sense of Intercultural Contact?: A Qualitative Study." In: *International Journal of Intercultural Relations,* 2008, 32, 1, 1–16.

Krewer, Bernd. "Interkulturelle Trainingsprogramme—Bestandsaufnahme und Perspektiven." In: *Nouveaux Cahiers d'Allemand,* 1994, 12, 2, 139-51.

da Silva, Vasco. Critical Incidents *in Spanien und Frankreich: Eine Evaluation studentischer Selbstanalysen.* Stuttgart: ibidem, 2010.

GO.INTERCULTURAL!
INTERCULTURAL TRAINING FOR UNIVERSITY STUDENTS
by Berenike Kuschel, Elke Bosse & Ioulia Grigorieva

Internationalization in Higher Education

UNTIL RECENTLY, THE few attempts to develop intercultural competence in German higher education institutions were limited to the initiative of individuals and were for the most part targeted at selected groups, *e.g.*, students participating in international Master's degree programs. It is only quite recently that German universities have begun to acknowledge the fact that internationalization produces more challenges than those of organizing student or staff mobility, developing international degree programs or creating marketing strategies to increase the number of international students. This is partly due to surveys that have revealed the lack of academic success and social integration of international students (Heublein *et al.* 2004), and new concepts that emphasize the need for "internationalization at home" (Crowther *et al.* 2000) have inspired a search for approaches that connect internationalization with intercultural learning on the level of the individual, and with development on the organizational level (Otten 2009).

In the course of this change, German higher education institutions have set up various projects that share a view of cultural diversity as a resource to be explored by the university as a whole. Local initiatives are supported at the national level by the German Academic Exchange Service (DAAD), with its special program to internationalize German higher education institutions (PROFIN).

One of the projects that have benefited from DAAD support is *Go.Intercultural!*, a student initiative at Hildesheim University that provides intercultural training for students. This article offers an introduction to this project, describing how it was established and how it complements the regular program of studies. The formal project evaluation has not been completed yet, but we will draw upon feedback from participants in order to illustrate some of the outcomes and the students' reactions.

Intercultural Communication at the University of Hildesheim

WITH ABOUT 5,600 students enrolled, Hildesheim University is by German standards rather a small college, but at the same time it has an exceptionally high rate of international mobility. This is due in particular to the largest faculty, Language and Information Studies. Within this faculty there is a well-established tradition of teaching intercultural communication. The degree program in International Information Management, for example, links information studies, comparative cultural studies and linguistic aspects of intercultural communication. This unique course design acknowledges the fact that intercultural aspects of information management and communication need to be addressed in order to meet the challenges of a globalized world.

While intercultural communication was originally only one of a number of core areas to be found within the former Department of Applied Linguistics, in 2009 the Institute of Intercultural Communication was established, confirming the special interest in this topic at Hildesheim University and the importance attached to it. Today the institute houses teachers and researchers from different cultural and linguistic backgrounds, with a wide range of intercultural experience, and academic expertise covering the fields of comparative cultural studies, cultural anthropology, second language acquisition and linguistics.

Go.Intercultural!—Intercultural Training for Students

THE STUDENTS' HIGH level of interest in intercultural communication is reflected not only in the number of participants enrolled in seminars on this topic but also in the foundation of the student initiative *Go.Intercultural!*—Intercultural Training for Students. In 2006 a group of students studying International Information Management set out to apply the theory they had learned in their seminars to practice. Their ambition was to carry out intercultural training workshops on a peer-to-peer basis in order to give students from any degree programs at Hildesheim University the chance to learn more about intercultural communication and to facilitate the development of intercultural competence. From the perspective of the peer trainers, designing and organizing intercultural workshops is an outstanding experience, which "helps a lot in regard to our professional orientation", as one of the participants has stated. After all, peer trainers welcome "the opportunity to apply theories of intercultural communication in a work-like context". Statements like these show that the students can benefit from their extracurricular engagement as peer trainers by gaining a first career orientation.

Qualification for Intercultural Communication

SINCE SPRING 2009 the students involved in *Go.Intercultural!* have no longer been alone in their endeavor. The project "Qualification for Intercultural Communication" (QUALIKO) initiated by the Institute of Intercultural Communication and funded by the DAAD as part of its program to internationalize German higher education institutions gives institutional support to the peer trainers. As the overall project goal is to foster inter-cultural learning on campus (Bosse 2009), Qualiko serves as a framework to integrate *Go.Intercultural!* into the process of internationalization of Hildesheim University. This is not just for practical reasons like providing the necessary infrastructure for carrying out workshops, but also to ensure a certain quality of the intercultural training program.

Quality control became an issue when the above-mentioned degree in International Information Management, a traditional German first-degree MA (*Magister*) program, received its last student intake and a new Bachelor program in the same subject was instituted. The BA students involved in *Go.Intercultural!* now only have very limited time to qualify as peer trainers in comparison to students in the *Magister* program. While *Magister* students study for four years or longer, the new BA degree is normally completed after three years, including at least one semester abroad. This leads to a high fluctuation of peer trainers, which would deeply affect the quality of both the theoretical foundation and the didactic approach of the work-shops—were it not for constant monitoring and counseling of the students.

This support is now provided by an adviser, who ensures detailed documentation of the workshops' contents and methods, meets regularly with the students to prepare and evaluate the workshops, and is also responsible for tasks like promoting the workshops, the registration of participants and the certification of attendance. As this adviser is a member of staff of the Institute of Intercultural Communication, quality and continuity in regard to the intercultural training program can be guaranteed and the student initiative forms an integral part of the institute's overall program of activities.

The Intercultural Training Program
at the University of Hildesheim

WHEN *GO.INTERCULTURAL!* first started, there was one basic training format, which consisted of a certain amount of theoretical input and a couple of interactive exercises. German students who would be going abroad and incoming international students were addressed as separate groups. QUALIKO then allowed further development of the intercultural training design, and now the program consists of a sequence of four separate two-day workshops conducted by students from the *Go.Intercultural!* initiative and by staff members from the Institute of Intercultural Communication. The workshops are open to students from every faculty of Hildesheim University, and they are all directed at both groups—local and international students—who are particularly interested in intercultural learning.

The design of each workshop combines experiential and didactic approaches to intercultural learning, creating space for students to exchange their intercultural experiences while providing the theoretical framework necessary for reflection. The didactic elements draw upon current research in the interdisciplinary field of intercultural communication, with an emphasis on intercultural pragmatics, which is a central topic of research interest within the Institute of Intercultural Communication at Hildesheim University. Using personal narratives, film-based critical incidents, simulation games and role plays, the workshops provide an insight into the challenges and opportunities of intercultural communication. The workshops' overall objectives are to enable students to broaden their intercultural experience, to explore the dynamics of intercultural encounters and to develop perspectives for actively engaging in intercultural communication. The training program is split into three modules that students can attend according to the phase of study that they are in.

The introductory module "International Campus" is

conducted by peer trainers, with the support of the adviser from the Institute of Intercultural Communication mentioned above. It is aimed at students in their initial stage of studies, as well as exchange students from abroad. The workshop is based on fundamental concepts from the field of intercultural communication that are introduced as tools for reflection and personal development, *e.g.*, students explore the meaning of different value orientations in connection with critical incidents on campus, they take part in a simulation game that highlights the dynamics of stereotyping, or they develop perspectives on how to improve cooperation between local and international students at the university. All these activities provide opportunities to get to know students from different cultural backgrounds and to work jointly on ideas on how to contribute to the internationalization of Hildesheim University. One former (German) student points out: "The workshop 'International Campus' encouraged me to help in support services for international students on our campus." For an international fulltime student from Sudan the workshop was a very important opportunity to meet German students. When asked for feedback he said that he often felt stared at on campus and that he thought that German students didn't dare to talk to him even though they wanted to. And he expressed his hopes that "now that I have met some German students they will greet me instead of staring at me".

The second module of the intercultural training program consists of two alternative workshops, "International Studies" and "International Internship", aimed at students who are preparing for or reflecting upon their stay abroad. These workshops deal with cultural differences with respect to studying or doing an internship abroad, address different teaching and learning styles as well as working styles, focus on intercultural communication at university or in the workplace, and cover the so-called "culture shock" phenomenon. Both workshops build upon the basic knowledge and skills of the first module, but shift the focus on concepts from cultural psychology and anthropology towards a linguistic perspective on intercultural communication. Using examples of everyday life on campus or in the workplace, the workshops illustrate divergent discourse conventions and their effects. Rather than merely providing "dos and don'ts", they seek to strengthen students' tolerance of ambiguity and their ability to analyze interaction in order to communicate according to their needs. The overall objective is the ability to detect differences on the level of communication, to avoid unintended effects of one's own communicative behavior and to avoid or repair possible misunderstandings.

"International Career", the third module, addresses students who are about to finish their studies and seek a career abroad or in Germany in an international organization or company where they are likely to work in intercultural teams or with international clients. The participants analyze their intercultural experiences as a possible resource for their future career, carry out self-assessment of their intercultural competence, explore possible challenges of working in intercultural teams, and practice presenting their experiences and skills in job interviews. The advantages of this approach are highlighted by one of the former participants, who says: "'International Career' confirmed my assumption that knowledge about intercultural communication is an important resource that we can really benefit from in working life."

During all the workshops students get to know a wide range of "tools" that will help them to analyze intercultural encounters and turn studying in an international environment into a profound learning experience. The insights that they gain range from a basic ability to reflect on their own cultural background to the acquisition of problem-solving strategies:

> We got lots of ideas about possible problems abroad and how we can solve them. Simulations and games helped us to find a critical perspective on our own culture and showed us how we interpret the behavior of members of foreign cultures.

Since the workshops combine theory and practice, even advanced students report learning effects that go beyond the knowledge that they acquired in their regular courses on intercultural communication. One participant says that she was pretty sure that she wouldn't learn anything new, but then came to realize with surprise that "knowing things and 'feeling' them are not the same". Most of the participants consider that they have increased their awareness of cultural differences by means of the workshops. For example, one student points out that "the workshop reminded me that cultural differences can be stressful, but also very inspiring". Another participant realized "that culture can be part of seemingly insignificant aspects which are part of everyday life so that one's own beliefs should be continuously put into perspective". The same person added: "You should be extremely attentive and careful with all kinds of signals, especially your own." All in all, these quotations show that the intercultural learning environment provided by the workshops may lead to very different individual insights that illustrate the various aspects and stages of intercultural competence development.

The Certificate in Intercultural Communication and Competence

THE QUALIKO PROJECT not only served as a framework for developing the training program described above; it also aimed to find ways of acknowledging intercultural qualification as a course-related or an extracurricular activity. Students receive a certificate of attendance for each of the workshops, and credits are awarded to ERASMUS exchange students as well as to local students in certain degree programs, provided that the intercultural training modules form an integral part of the curriculum.

As this only applies to a rather small number of students, QUALIKO sets out to create a special incentive for *all* students at Hildesheim University to increase their active engagement with intercultural communication and learning. As a result, the

Certificate in Intercultural Communication and Competence was developed. In addition to participation in the intercultural training program as a means of furthering intercultural reflection, it takes into account students' intercultural experience acquired during stays abroad or through language courses as well as their active involvement in support services for international students, working for *Go.Intercultural!* being one of the recognized forms of engagement with intercultural communication. (Another form of intercultural reflection acknowledged by the certificate is the Portfolio in Intercultural Communication and Competence (PIKK), see DA SILVA in this volume.)

Introduced towards the end of 2009 and with approximately 120 students registered within its first year, the certificate has proven useful in demonstrating that there is more to intercultural competence development than international mobility. Students who are interested in the certificate receive individual counseling on how to broaden their insights into intercultural communication and how to widen their profile during the course of their studies. In this way, the certificate not only supports the idea of internationalization at home, motivating students to make use of the many oportunities for intercultural communication on campus; it also contributes to the students' future employability, an objective that has gained in importance since three-year Bachelor degree programs were phased in at German universities—in the context of the so-called "Bologna Process" of the European Union—to replace the traditional four-to-five-year first-degree programs (*Magister*, *Diplom*, and so on).

Train-the-Trainer Workshops for Peer Trainers

AS MENTIONED ABOVE, the peer trainers of *Go.Intercultural!* are responsible for the introductory workshop and therefore receive a special preparation in tutoring thanks to QUALIKO. In addition to this, and the regular seminar courses on the design of intercultural training offered by lecturers from the Institute of Intercultural Communication, QUALIKO prepares the members of *Go.Intercultural!* for their role as intercultural trainers through the format of train-the-trainer workshops. On the one hand this serves as a means of teambuilding and an opportunity to integrate new members of *Go.Intercultural!*. On the other hand it allows an exchange with students from similar initiatives at other German universities who are also invited to take part in the two-day workshops. The train-the-trainer workshops therefore provide not only theoretical input, based on the latest academic research; they also enable the peer trainers to compare and revise their intercultural training design and to exchange knowledge, experiences and material on training activities.

Over the last three years a network has been created within which similarly-minded German initiatives support and encourage each other. One participant from Berlin, for example, expressed her appreciation of the "exchange of ideas, know-how and best practice in areas such as content, methods and acquisition of workshop participants and peer trainers", welcoming the opportunity of "coaching less experienced peer trainers".

Applied Research and Development

A NUMBER OF students at Hildesheim's Institute of Intercultural Communication have conducted—and are still carrying out—research on various aspects of internationalization and intercultural communication on campus for their degree thesis. For example, there have been empirical studies on the academic and social integration of exchange students at Hildesheim University (Bartelt 2010; Reich 2010) or on the design and outcomes of mentoring programs for international students (Söffker 2010). One graduate emphasized her appreciation of her thesis being a "part of a bigger idea of internationalization at home" and found it motivating that her survey had contributed directly to the objectives of the QUALIKO project. Another graduate underlined the direct relevance of her topic to students' everyday lives, seeing her work as a way of gaining a better understanding of the needs of international and local students.

This kind of applied research relating to Hildesheim University can only serve to improve and readjust the existing opportunities for intercultural qualification that are currently on offer. Another means of generating suggestions for intercultural development is the exchange of ideas between experts and practitioners in the field of intercultural communication organized by QUALIKO. For example, in 2009 the Institute of Intercultural Communication hosted a conference on qualitative methods in the field of intercultural communication, which addressed both fundamental research issues and the potential contribution that qualitative research can make to the ongoing process of internationalization in higher education institutions. Additionally, every semester there are colloquia on QUALIKO-related issues held at Hildesheim University which address such questions as the recognition of extra-curricular intercultural qualifications, the application of e-portfolios to document and reflect the development of intercultural competence, and matters of intercultural qualification in teaching, counseling and research. Not only experts are invited to these meetings, but also members of *Go.Intercultural!*, who, according to one participant, appreciate "the opportunity to gain valuable insights into current research projects in the field of intercultural communication".

Conclusion

JUDGING BY THE positive comments and the increasing number of participants (growing from thirty, when the modules for intercultural training were first introduced, to 160 in 2010), the institutionalization and diversification of opportunities for intercultural learning at Hildesheim University has been an outstanding success. Through the projects and activities outlined above, internationalization has advanced beyond straightforward mobility, enabling students to appreciate that "experience itself does not teach; people learn from reflecting on their experience" (Tjosvold 1991, 189).

Nevertheless there are still a number of open questions that need to be addressed in the future. One question, for instance, is how to reach students from *all* faculties, as up to now most of the participants have come from the Faculty of Language and Information Studies. And—it would surely make sense to offer intercultural qualification opportunities not only to students but also to academic and administrative staff, in order to involve the university as a whole in the process of internationalization.

One might also want to ask, on a more general level, whether all the reflection and preparation described above only destroys the charm of "encountering the other". Instead of helping students to cope with cultural differences, it might even hinder their unbiased contact with others. Could a more naïve approach perhaps be advantageous, because the extensive analysis of differences clouds the view and handicaps the students rather than supports them? Don't intercultural training programs actually invite criticism as being not much more than a mere "culture shock prevention industry" (Hannerz 1992, 251)? Skeptical viewpoints of this kind notwithstanding, we doubt very much that nowadays there *can* be a naïve approach to intercultural interaction. Modern media and increased mobility confront us constantly with images that need to be questioned if they are not to turn into stereotypes. Therefore, internationalization in higher education should not rely solely on spontaneous experiential learning, but should be accompanied by systematic guidance to facilitate the development of intercultural competence.

References

Bartelt, Inga. *Integration und Kooperation von internationalen und deutschen Studierenden—Eine Untersuchung am Beispiel der Universität Hildesheim.* Unpublished *Magister* thesis, 2010.

Bosse, Elke. "Intercultural Training and Development at Hildesheim University, Germany." In: *Intercultural Education*, 20, 5, 2009, 485-89.

Crowther, Paul / Joris, Michael / Otten, Matthias / Nilsson,

Bengt / Teekens, Hanneke / Wächter, Bernd. *Internationalization at Home: A Position Paper*. Amsterdam: EAIE, 2000. Website, <http://www.eaie.org/IaH/IaHPositionPaper.pdf>

Hannerz, Ulf. *Cultural Complexity*. New York: Columbia University Press, 1992.

Heublein, Ulrich / Sommer, Dieter / Weitz, Brigitta. *Studienverlauf im Ausländerstudium: Eine Untersuchung an vier ausgewählten Hochschulen*. Bonn: DAAD, 2004.

Methodische Vielfalt in der Erforschung interkultureller Kommunikation an deutschen Hochschulen (Conference at the Institute of Intercultural Communication, Hildesheim University, 15.-17.10.2010). Website, <http://www.uni-hildesheim.de/ikk2009/>

Otten, Matthias. "*Academicus interculturalis?*: Negotiating interculturality in academic communities of practice." In: *Intercultural Education*, 20, 5, 2009, 407-17.

"Programm zur Förderung der Integration ausländischer Studierender (PROFIN)." In: *Deutscher Akademischer Austausch Dienst (DAAD)*, 2010. Website, <http://www.daad.de/hoch-schulen/betreuung/profin/09239.de.html>

Reich, Sabine. *Die akademische und soziale Integration von ERASMUS-Studierenden: Eine Untersuchung am Beispiel der Universität Hildesheim*. Unpublished *Magister* thesis, 2010.

Söffker, Marieke. *Mentorenprogramme für internationale Studierende: Bedarf und Konzeption am Beispiel der Universität Hildesheim*. Unpublished *Magister* thesis, 2010.

Tjosvold, Dean. *Team organization: An enduring competitive advantage*. Chichester, W. Sussex: John Wiley & Sons, 1990.

BIOGRAPHICAL RESEARCH
AN INTERCULTURAL APPROACH?
by HELENA DRAWERT

Introduction

COLLECTING, ANALYZING AND saving biographical data from a
scholarly perspective and using systematic qualitative research
methods, particularly in sociology, is still quite a young field
of research, even though it draws upon a long tradition of
biography and its notation goes back to ancient times (Alheit
/ Dausin 1990, 16; Fischer-Rosenthal 1990, 14). It has gained
in importance and obtained acceptance in various academic
disciplines and in connection with different research objectives,
particularly during the last thirty years. Globalization, modern-
ization and differentiation within postmodern society, plural-
ization of lifestyles and the dissolution of traditional values
have all underlined the urgent need for biographical research
today. In times characterized by global challenges it is important to obtain an understanding of the human being and his or
her point of view and place in society, in terms of intercultural
dimensions and changes too.

However, with regard to the increasing cultural diversity and
varied intercultural objectives in modern society biographical
research still leaves a lot to be desired, although its proponents
have taken to referring to its importance for "intercultural fields
of research". Rita Franceschini (2001), for example, asserts: "To
analyse interculturality from the viewpoint of biography—or

biography from that of interculturality—is a research perspective which has proved productive, but also challenging" (8).

This essay will consider the question of analyzing (intercultural) phenomena by using qualitative and especially biographical research methods, with particular emphasis on the autobiographical narrative interview approach.

Brief Historical Survey of Biographical Research Methods

THE "SPECIFIC MODERN importance" of biography arose with the development in Europe, between the fourteenth and eighteenth centuries, of a "middle-class individual" (*Herausbildung des bürgerlichen Individuums*, Alheit / Dausin, 7). During the Enlightenment, biography became of general interest first in philosophy and the humanities, later (as the separate disciplines became more distinct) in specific areas like literature. Biographical notation was reconditioned by the emergence of different types of corporate self-expression, such as biographies of citizens and tradesmen, memoirs of the military, and biographies of artists and scholars (Fischer-Rosenthal, 14). The biographical genre was already long since self-contained, culminating in the publication of Goethe's biography *Dichtung und Wahrheit* (1811-1831).

Later, there were biographical writings from the bourgeoisie or from the proletariat (in relation to the labor movement). However, these writings weren't published and analyzed (that happened later) from a social scientific or socio-political perspective. Besides this, biographies of influential personalities were published, for example biographies of Engels (by Gustav Meyers, 1919, 1932) and Marx (by Franz Mehring, 1918). Biography proved to be a suitable medium not only for analyzing political and social processes, for instance in connection with the labor movement, but also for analyzing different cultural phenomena from the point of view of anthropology and ethnology, *e.g.*, the European immigrants in America (Fischer-Rosenthal, 15). The scholarly utilization of biographical data (particularly in the field of sociology) was an achievement of the Twenties. Biographical research began at the University of Chicago with the migration study *The Polish Peasant in Europe and America* by William Isaac Thomas and Florian Znaniecki (1918-20). It was the first instance of biographical field research in sociology, pioneering an approach that made contemplation of the subjective viewpoint of a human being the central object of research.

During the Thirties further qualitative field research was undertaken, in particular by Ernest W. Burgess and Robert E. Park, who were building up the "Chicago School" of sociology at that time. But in the following years biographical research suffered some ups and downs, on the one hand because of such changes as the increase in the use of quantitative methods, and on the other for historical and political reasons. During the Second World War, for example, biographical research was somewhat restricted—especially in Germany, where "central ideological elements of National Socialism, particularly the doctrines of race and heredity, were contrary to 'biographical' thinking" (Fuchs-Heinritz, 112).

After the war, biographical research was on the upswing again. During the Sixties and Seventies it fully emerged as an approach, and was enhanced by Oral History in historical sciences and the Life History Approach in sociology. The "boom" of the last two decades of the twentieth century has been ascribed, among other things, to individualization and change in social structure and society.

It is not surprising, therefore, that much qualitative-interpretive research, and especially biographical analysis, does not presuppose social normality but rather asks about experiences during times of social transformation and in moments and times of crisis, and the emergence of needs for new social practices to prevent further exclusion or the complete breakdown of individual or social life (Apitzsch / Inowlocki 2000, 7).

Werner Fuchs-Heinritz (2009, 121 f.) points to two further factors: firstly, the wish to save the biographical data of contemporary witnesses (for example memories of war, but also cultural experiences and memories of endangered ethnic groups like the North American Indians), and secondly, technical innovations. The invention of the tape-recorder enormously facilitated data collection in the context of qualitative research in the social sciences, and the autobiographical narrative interview method was one of the beneficiaries. The method achieved a high profile in a number of different disciplines and can still be described as a central surveying technique in biographical research.

Autobiographical Narrative Interviews in Qualitative Research

THE AUTOBIOGRAPHICAL NARRATIVE interview was developed in the late Seventies in Germany by the sociologist Fritz Schütze (1983, 1987), who also established this method in qualitative social research. In connection with a survey at the University of Bielefeld about communal power structures (Schütze 1977), Schütze used the interview as a method of collecting biographical data for the first time.

The autobiographical narrative interview basically depends on stories about life(stages) of a real person of interest. It utilizes "authentic" narratives of people with different thematic focuses. Looking beyond sociology, it is therefore a useful tool in other disciplines such as educational science, psychology, anthropology, and even cultural studies and intercultural research. They all share an interest in the subject and its role in society. Through the story told in the interview the researcher becomes part of social and (inter)cultural phenomena of interest. Personal narratives reveal (inter)cultural and social patterns through individual experiences (Patton, 115 f.).

Life stories and personal narratives are increasingly being used in a wide range of disciplines and settings. Whether it is for research purposes on a particular topic or question or to learn more about human lives and society in general ways from one person's perspective, life stories serve as excellent means for understanding how people see their own experiences, their own lives, and their interactions with others (Atkinson 1998, 74).

The method of the autobiographical narrative interview as described here is also important in linguistics. Research into authentic language, or rather into the linguistic presentation of life, is essential for being able to draw conclusions about social relations. Often, contents of particular interest are revealed specifically through language, through the way they are expressed.

Life stories can also be used to explain and define relationships and group memberships, especially in regard to language used to do so. The stories people tell about their lives all contain discourse units, degrees of coherence, and an overall linguistic structure, all of which are useful in determining the relation between language and social practice, the relation of self to others, and the creation of social identity (Atkinson, 14, see also Lindem 1993 and Mkhonza 1995).

This is of utmost significance for cultural studies and intercultural research too, when considering how intercultural dimensions and aspects of life are expressed in biography and brought out and reflected in language—through the autobiographical interview. As it is a great challenge to get at this narrative, the autobiographical narrative interview follows a sequence of steps in collecting (and evaluating) data.

The Autobiographical Narrative Interview Method

IT IS AN important principle in narrative interviews that the main narrative is produced independently by the interviewee.

The main narrative is initiated by an opening narrative-generating question, inviting the interviewee to mobilize memories, for instance: "What's the story of your life, tell me about it!" This demand often provokes a response that reflects the interviewee's uncertainty: "Shall I simply tell you my story? What do you want to know?"

Following on from this, the interviewer will ideally elicit a main narrative or self-structured biographical self-presentation from the interviewee: "Tell me everything you want to tell and what comes into your mind!" The "flowing", independently produced main narrative is the most important part of the interview, and is accompanied by active listening, supportive gestures, non-directive comments and note-taking by the interviewer. When this main period finds its "natural end", marked by the interviewee with comments like: "Well, that's life! Yes, that's how it was!", a period with internal narrative questions will then follow.

These questions are based on the notes taken during the interview so far. They generate further stories ("Could you be more specific about the situation you were talking about in the interview?"). After that and if so desired the interviewer can ask so-called external narrative questions with the help of a prepared questionnaire (for further information about this, see Schütze 1983).

This interview method is suitable for eliciting authentic narrative, supplemented by the responses to a standardized questionnaire. It represents a great potential resource for systematic researching of the individual perspective, with reference to various areas of social life. It can also be seen as a significant way of approaching the question of the systematic exploration of the subjective side of interculturality in intercultural fields of research.

Schütze's work and the autobiographical narrative interview method are based on findings in linguistics, narratology, ethnography and cultural studies, but always with an interdisciplinary orientation. The importance of narrative in empirical research into communication in everyday life remains Schütze's main area of interest—with obvious applications to intercultural research as well. His work has been strongly influenced by interpretative North American sociology, and in particular by ethnomethodology, conversation analysis, socio-linguistics and the concepts of major sociologists like Alfred Schütz (phenomenology), George Herbert Mead (symbolic interactionism), Anselm Strauss and Barney Glaser (grounded theory), and others. The development of such qualitative research methods as the autobiographical narrative interview, particularly within biographical research, is the result of various influencing factors.

> Maintaining strong relations with Northern American and Western European theoretical traditions is neither an accidental nor a recent phenomenon. The background and productiveness of the qualitative-interpretive approach, especially within biographical research [...] derives its characteristics and potential rather from a history of import and export and re-importing of thought, and also from a process of migration. This is exemplified in the work of Alfred Schütz, Georg Simmel and Karl Mannheim, which first became prominent in the United States after the Second World War, before it became a major influence in qualitative-interpretative sociology in Europe (Apitzsch / Inowlocki, 6).

It is interesting that the biographical approach within social research has such an intercultural background, evolving as it did at the cross-continental intersection of varying traditions. Just as the development of theoretical qualitative traditions, of which biographical research forms a part, has an intercultural dimension, so too might the objects and interests of biographical research be intercultural.

Biographical Research as an Intercultural Approach

IN THE LIGHT of the social changes and increasing cultural diversity in times of globalization, international networking and mobility and migration processes, qualitative research into the individual and his or her living environment and status in society is becoming more and more important. Understanding and explaining the intercultural interaction between humans in society can only be guaranteed if we turn to those directly concerned. Analyzing intercultural phenomena via qualitative research methods with reference to the individual implies the possibility of creating a better understanding of cultural diversity and intercultural living together in modern society. It is important to listen to the people directly involved in intercultural experiences, for example in processes of migration and in discussions about integration.

> For similar reasons, because how we tell our stories is mediated by our culture (Josselson 1995), we need to hear the life stories of individuals from those underrepresented groups to help establish a balance in literature and expand the options for us all on the cultural level (Atkinson, 19).

Biographical research by way of the autobiographical narrative interview provides a scholarly approach that can enrich the study of cultural diversity and intercultural coherences and teach us more about culture. The story of life or life phases, presented in the words of the person telling it, grants access to individual points of view, also with regard to intercultural aspects.

> A life story is a fairly complete narrating of one's entire experience of life as a whole, highlighting the

most important aspects. A life story gives us the vantage point of seeing how one person experiences and understands life, his or her own especially, over time (8).

If intercultural experiences, for example because of social changes or movements of migration and immigration in different contexts, are a highlight of one's biography, then this is an important field of biographical research. This is hardly surprising, keeping in mind that immigration and migration in particular often lead to drastic breaks in people's lives. These can be analyzed through the life story itself and the person telling it.

An individual life, and the role it plays in the larger community, is best understood through story. We become fully aware, fully conscious, of our own lives through the process of putting them together in story form. It is through story that we gain context and recognize meaning. Reclaiming story is part of our birthright. Telling our story enables us to be heard, recognized and acknowledged by others. Story makes the implicit explicit, the hidden seen, the unformed formed, and the confusing clear (7).

To sum up, (life)storytelling is an everyday competence within a systematic approach of biographical research which grants direct access to the living environment of individuals as social actors—and therefore to subjective intercultural experiences imbedded in social contexts.

Conclusion

BIOGRAPHIES REVEAL INDIVIDUAL life stories, and make these and the intercultural aspects of people's lives accessible. They also disclose the living environment of individuals and/or groups, their individual and partial or collective interests, and their social status. Biographies also detect collective standards and attitudes in society and clarify changes, especially in connection with intercultural objectives. "To analyse interculturality from the viewpoint of biography—or biography from that of interculturality" definitely provides a productive line of research. And it should be stressed, as Franceschini (2001, 8) points out, that biographical research with intercultural objectives needs to be aware of the importance of interdisciplinarity. Different disciplines with different traditions, expectations and questions approach the nexus of biography and interculturality in different ways, constituting a rich research resource. Biographical research can be enriched by different research methods, like for example those from an ethnographic perspective. This diversity and interdisciplinarity will be needed for exploring interculturality within biography and *vice versa*.

References

Alheit, Peter / Dausin, Bettina. *Biographie: Eine problemgeschichtliche Skizze (Werkstattberichte des Forschungsschwerpunkts "Arbeit und Bildung", 14)*. Bremen: Universität Bremen, 1990.

Apitzsch, Ursula / Inowlocki, Lena. "Biographical Analysis: A 'German' School?" In: *Biographical Research Methods*. Ed. Robert Lee Miller. Volume III. Thousand Oaks, CA: Sage, 2005, 5-23.

Atkinson, Robert. *The Life Story Interview*. Thousand Oaks, CA: Sage, 1998.

Fischer-Rosenthal, Wolfram. "Von der 'biographischen Methode' zur Biographieforschung: Versuch einer Standortbestimmung." In: *Biographieforschung: Eine Zwischenbilanz in der deutschen Soziologie*. Ed. Peter Alheit / Wolfram Fischer-Rosenthal / Erika M. Hoernig. Bremen: Universität Bremen, 1990, 11-32.

Franceschini, Rita (Ed.). *Biographie und Interkulturalität*:

Diskurs und Lebenspraxis. Tübingen: Stauffenburg, 2001.

Fuchs-Heinritz, Werner. *Biographische Forschung: Eine Einführung in Praxis und Methoden*. Fourth edition. Wiesbaden: VS Verlag für Sozialwissenschaften, 2009.

Goethe, Johann Wolfgang von. *Aus meinem Leben: Dichtung und Wahrheit*. (1811-31). Fourth edition. Berlin: Aufbau, 1981.

Josselson, Ruthellen. "Imagining the Real: Empathy, Narrative, and the Dialogic Self." In: *The Narrative Study of Lives*. Ed. Ruthellen Josselson / Amia Lieblich. Volume 3. Thousand Oaks, CA:. Sage, 1995, 27-44.

Lindem, Charlotte. *Life Stories: The Creation of Coherence*. New York: Oxford University Press, 1993.

Mkhonza, Sarah. "Life Histories as Social Texts of Personal Experiences in Sociolinguistic Studies: A Look at the Lives of Domestic Workers in Swaziland." In: *The Narrative Study of Lives*, 173-204.

Patton, Michael Quinn. *Qualitative Research and Evaluation Methods*. Third edition. Thousand Oaks, CA: Sage, 2001.

Schütze, Fritz. *Die Technik des narrativen Interviews in Interaktionsfeldstudien—dargestellt an einem Projekt zur Erforschung von kommunalen Machtstrukturen*. Bielefeld: Manuskript, 1977.

------------. "Biographieforschung und narratives Interview." In: *Neue Praxis: Kritische Zeitschrift für Sozialarbeit und Sozialpädagogik*, 13, 3, 1983, 283-93.

------------. *Das narrative Interview in Interaktionsfeldstudien: Erzähltheoretische Grundlagen*. Hagen: Fernuniversität, 1987.

Thomas, Wiliam I. / Znaniecki, Florian. *The Polish Peasant in Europe and America* (1918-20). Abridged version. Urbana: University of Illinois, 1996.

NOTE: The English translations of quotations from the German works listed above are by the author.

USING SOCIAL INFORMATION AND COMMUNICATION TOOLS TO FOSTER INTERCULTURAL EXCHANGE AND LEARNING

by JOACHIM GRIESBAUM

IT IS WIDELY believed that modern information and communication technology can play a vital part in fostering intercultural exchange and learning (O'Dowd 2007a, 2007b, *etc.*). The rise of the Web 2.0, or more precisely a social web with huge scope for participation (Shirky 2008), has often been seen as a quantum leap offering unparalleled opportunities to initiate and enhance intercultural exchange and learning in educational contexts. This article aims to give a basic overview of the possibilities of using (social) information and communication technology (ICT) for intercultural learning. It presents some ideas and concepts that are currently being developed in Hildesheim for using social software as a tool to initiate and foster intercultural learning and exchange in higher education. The paper closes with a look into the future and some thoughts about the limits of intercultural learning and exchange in online environments.

Intercultural Exchange and Learning

CULTURE IS ONE of the many factors determining human perception, thinking and behavior (Samovar *et al.* 2010, 22-24). Culture is learned, cultivated within and shared by a group of people. It consists of various factors and acts as an interpretive frame of behavior (Dahl 2004). A globalized world requires communication and information flows that overcome language and cultural barriers (Krishna *et al.* 2004). Thus today's students urgently need to acquire the knowledge and skills required for communicating interculturally.

In higher education, intercultural communication competence is usually acquired in study programs. In addition, international structures like the ERASMUS program of the European Commission or national organizations like the German Academic Exchange Service (DAAD) facilitate study, research and teaching abroad (see DA SILVA, in this volume).

E-Learning and Social Software

KAHIIGI *ET AL.* (2008) give an overview of the current state of E-Learning and define it as the application of ICT for learning purposes. The aim of E-Learning is to increase the efficiency and effectiveness of learning processes. Implementation strategies are dependent on factors like the degree of virtuality, technology use, didactic design principles, content *vs.* process orientation and learner *vs.* instructor centrism. Technologies range from learning management systems (LMS) and content management systems (CMS) to multimedia communities and virtual worlds. In the last ten years, E-Learning has been established as a standard in higher education. Concrete arrangements are usually defined by instructors. Thus E-Learning provides a multitude of opportunities to create new, more flexible learning scenarios. Nevertheless, with regard to the adequate use of technology or the implementation of didactic learning arrangements it is still in its infancy, and generally restricted by the capabilities of instructors and the structures predefined by them. There is a lot of room for improvement and a continued need for further research.

Within the context of Web 2.0 there has emerged a discussion of new paradigms in E-Learning. Web 2.0 is an umbrella term for technological and social trends in the internet that focus on new forms of user participation and user-generated content (O'Reilly 2005). Users perceive and use the internet in new ways. They are no longer primarily restricted to consuming content published by professionals, but are increasingly participating in forums, blogs, *etc.*, and forming new kinds of social communities in social online networks like (for example) Facebook. An increasing range of user-friendly social software and media facilitate the publishing of content and offer manifold opportunities for networking. As Shirky argues, a new social web is lowering the barriers of knowledge sharing and communication, thus changing the ecosystem of human society by making once-impossible forms of publishing and group action possible. As the title (*Here Comes Everybody*) suggests, *everyone is a media outlet* and the social web empowers users to *organize without organizations*. So it can be argued that the emergence of a social web has expanded the possibilities for communication and collaboration. Public communication, once largely controlled by gatekeepers such as the print media or television, is now a more open space in which potentially everyone can participate through tools like blogs, wikis, podcasts, and so on. Cooperation and collaboration, which were previously usually bound to and enabled by the organizational framework of institutions or enterprises, now often happen *ad hoc*, no longer requiring steady involvement and external coordination. Wikipedia and the open source movement are examples of such open cooperation processes.

After this short digression on Web 2.0 and the social web, we should consider the meaning of the term "E-Learning 2.0". This expression was coined by Downes (2005) in differentiation and criticism of previous E-Learning practices, which are described and judged with a knowledge transfer metaphor. According to Downes, such E-Learning 1.0 scenarios are characterized by "docent centrism" (meaning that they are usually controlled and predetermined by the instructor) and by the transfer of "learning objects" (knowledge as an "object") as a primary learning goal. Furthermore, they are often supported (or rather limited) by closed LMS, in which the possibilities of communication and publishing for learners are predefined and often restricted. Such LMS could be described as closed or isolated islands that only reproduce classroom walls in virtual space. This is contrasted with a picture of a new generation of learners ("digital natives", Prensky 2001), who should be accustomed to actively participating in online conversations and in the forming of online communities. For this new generation of learners the provision of tools like E-Portfolios or blogs as a means for publishing, interacting and learning together in open communities, not limited to a given social group, such as a university class, would be much more appropriate. In summary, Downes points out that social media can be seen as an infrastructure to foster free, *i.e.,* potentially unrestricted, many-to-many communication and knowledge exchange in educational contexts. Baumgartner (2006) proposes the use of social software a) as a didactic tool to support and allow specific didactic scenarios, for example E-Portfolios as an assessment tool, and b) as an institutional infrastructure, primarily supporting informal learning.

Focusing on this last point, employing social software in higher education can be interpreted from a knowledge management perspective as a means of fostering social interaction to support individual and social learning. Griesbaum / Kepp (2010) argue that social software should be employed as a social information and communication infrastructure, thus enabling new possibilities for manifold knowledge (exchange and creation) processes across personal and organizational boundaries within (and potentially also outside) the institution.

The Use of Information and Communication Technology in Intercultural Exchange and Learning

RITCHIE (2009), O'Dowd (2007a) and O'Dowd (2007b) offer a survey of E-Learning in the field of intercultural exchange and learning, showing that there is a broad range in which information and communication technologies are applied. Most use cases can be categorized as formal learning settings, in which the instructors provide and configure a social and technological learning environment within classes or between classes from different locations. Learning scenarios are often focused on language learning, for example second language acquisition. By bringing together learners from different languages, computer-mediated communication tools provide interactive access to language and culture in context, something that is not accessible in the traditional classroom (Ritchie, 26). Especially in scenarios that connect native speakers with non-native speakers, participants are motivated for mutual interaction and knowledge exchange. Furthermore, learners are motivated in collaborative discourse (Savignon / Rothmeier 2004). According to Lee (2004), who investigated open-ended online discussion between native speakers and non-native speakers of Spanish studying in US institutions, text-based chat promotes collaborative linguistic scaffolding between the two groups. Chan *et al.* (2007) formed virtual teams of US and Australian students who had to coordinate their schedules and activities with the help of the voice-over IP tool Skype. Results of the study indicate that students were successfully exposed to diverse perspectives from their peers. Davis / Thiede (2000) report results from a study in which forums were used for discussions between native speakers and non-native speakers of English. They concluded that the asynchronous discussions fostered reflection on language use. Other studies (Law *et al.* 2007, Aoki / Kimura 2009, O'Dowd 2007b) that combine multiple online communication, partly also including social software like blogs, wikis, social networks (Facebook), report encouraging results, too.

Dervin (2007) states that

> with the birth of Web 2.0 technologies and applications (Facebook, Skype, Twitter, Flickr...), unparalleled possibilities have opened up for language and intercultural education. Instead of the static cyberspace, this living web is user-centered and urges people to share information, collaborate, network, create, manipulate...(1).

He describes possible use cases of social media for intercultural learning. Social media may be used a) for working with data and ideas and b) for the involvement with others. Examples of a) include tools such as social bookmarking (*e.g.*, delicious.com) that may be employed to access and share knowledge resources, online office (*e.g.*, 280slides.com) to create and share knowledge artefacts like presentations or to collect and represent words, ideas, tasks (*e.g.*, bubbl.us). Examples of b) cover social networking (*e.g.*, facebook.com) or microblogging (*e.g.*, twitter.com). That means that, according to Dervin, social media transfer intercultural learning to a new level by providing newly available tools, which support and facilitate (personal) knowledge and information management and at the same time widen the scope and chances for socially constructed learning (Vygotsky 1979). Both arguments make sense if one takes into account the qualities that are usually expected of social software: to be easily accessible by everyone and producing positive network effects by linking people even in contexts where the primary user intent is individual-based (*e.g.*, the management of links in social bookmark services), thus providing diverse possibilities and occasions for many-to-many communication and cooperation.

It can be concluded that the use of ICT in general and social media in particular can to be very rewarding in promoting socially constructed exchange and knowledge construction of dislocated learners. Therefore E-Learning seems to be a very worthwhile endeavor to foster learning effectiveness, at least as far as language acquisition is concerned. It is important to note that these results should not be interpreted as merely techno-centric. In formal learning scenarios, the teacher's role, his ability and his design choices regarding the construction of online interaction are of uppermost importance. This means that technology is only one of many factors determining inputs and outputs of learning scenarios.

So far we have focused on formal learning scenarios, just as the vast majority of literature does. As argued above, social media can not only be seen as appropriate tools to support formal learning but also as an opportunity to provide an easily accessible and participative infrastructure for informal learning and knowledge management. *Tandem language learning*, a setup in which dyads of native speakers of different languages practice mutual exchange, is a typical scenario of less formal or informal learning in this field. Babelyou.com is a service that supports E-Tandems for everyone. Interested learners get the opportunity to search for partners, to create so-called learning rooms and to get in computer-mediated contact with partners. There is even a possibility to publish travelogues to foster inter-cultural experiences and understanding. Apart from such initia-tives, there is currently little use of participative social media in the field of intercultural exchange and learning. Organizations concerned with academic exchange programs use ICT primarily for one-to-many information distribution purposes, *e.g.*, the Belgian American Education Foundation (baef.be), the German Academic Exchange Service (daad.de), the ERASMUS program of the European Commission (eacea.ec.europa.eu), or the Board of European Students of Technology (best.eu.org). Some initia-tives at least—for instance, the ERASMUS Student Network (helpcenter.esn.org) or the AEGEE (European Students' Forum, aegee.org)—offer many-to-many communication platforms or are even actively involved in social networks (facebook.com/aegee). Infrastructures and services that initiate and execute direct (face-to-face, or virtual) intercultural communication and exchange on a high social level currently employ ICT primarily for one-to-many information distribution purposes. The same often applies to local organizations at the university level. For example, the website of the International Office at the University of Hildesheim offers a wealth of information both for *incoming* and for *outgoing* students, but only an internal forum for many-to-many communication and knowledge creation purposes. Forum access is mainly restricted to university members (outgoings). This means that foreign students who may possibly be interested in the University of Hildesheim are not included in this kind of peer-to-peer communication.

To sum up, we have seen that using information and communication technology in intercultural exchange and E-Learning can be very worthwhile and is partly established in formal learning scenarios. On a broader social level, assessed from an information and communication infrastructure perspective, we may conclude that the potential of the social web for easy involvement, open communication and free participation has not yet been widely realized. The information distribution paradigm is still prevalent and public communication flows are still controlled by traditional gatekeepers or professional organizations.

Concepts and Ideas Currently
Being Tested at the University of Hildesheim

AT THE UNIVERSITY of Hildesheim there are experiments currently going on to use social information and communication tools to foster intercultural exchange and learning. In the summer semester of 2009, the idea and concept of applying software as a personal and social information and communication infrastructure in higher education was presented to a group of students in a seminar on "collaborative knowledge management". During the semester, the students on this course designed and configured a prototype of such a system on the basis of their own needs and ideas. They started with an analysis of the requirements and the identification of use cases for such an environment. The next task was the selection of the software that would serve as a technological basis. Several open source systems were compared—including Drupal (drupal.org), Elgg (elgg.org), and Stud.IP (studip.de). In the end, Mahara (mahara. org), an E-Portfolio software with social network features, was chosen, installed and configured. In a meeting of the whole group the name "CollabUni" was suggested for the project, and approved by a large majority of the participants. Using this low-cost and bottom-up approach, students succeeded in drafting and implementing a basic system that provides the essential features of a personal and social information and communication infrastructure as described above, *i.e.*, with possibilities for self-determined self-representation, networking and many-to-many communication. Hence, users can create profiles and views containing information about themselves. For each view, users can determine whether it should be accessible for everyone on the web, only to CollabUni users, only to contacts, or only to people who are invited. Besides direct data input, users can upload or embed files, integrate and aggregate RSS feeds, and maintain blogs on their profile page or views. Thus CollabUni offers E-Portfolio functionality, because it can be used to collect and reflect on achievements, objectives, *etc.* In addition, CollabUni can be used to connect to other people through contacts or groups. Groups can be created by every CollabUni user. They offer the functionality to build group views and forums. Thus, collaborative learning spaces can be created for the sharing of individual contents, co-construction of group contents and communication through the use of forums.

With respect to fostering intercultural exchange and learning, CollabUni is currently employed as a tool to support a) domestic students going abroad ("outgoings") as well as b) foreign ERASMUS exchange students visiting the University of Hildesheim ("incomings").

Regarding the outgoing students, the Institute of Intercultural Communication offers a certificate in intercultural communication and competence which acknowledges formal and informal learning. The certificate not only serves as an incentive for students to apply for mobility programs and to engage in support services for international students, it also provides students with the opportunity to document and reflect upon their intercultural experience abroad (Bosse 2009, KUSCHEL *et al.* in this volume). Collabuni is therefore applied as a tool that supports accompanied intercultural learning. As far as social information and communication are concerned, learners themselves are able to determine if and with whom they share their portfolio, and their learning processes (see also DA SILVA in this volume).

Regarding the incoming students, CollabUni may be used to support them through a community that facilitates the establishing of contacts between exchange students among themselves as well as with domestic students. In the summer semester of 2010 another group of students in a further seminar on "collaborative knowledge management" designed and planned an exchange student community within CollabUni. In general experience, ERASMUS exchange students mainly keep among themselves. Beyond university introductory events and welcome programs, ongoing contacts between ERASMUS and domestic students tend to be rather sparse. But a community offers free many-to-many communication. That means that the static information provided by the International Office can be supplemented with shared contents provided directly by peers.

The students decided to use English as a *lingua franca* and provided a default set of contents. To enrich the mass of information already provided by the International Office with respect to formal aspects of the ERASMUS program and curricula at the university, the new information focuses on social life in Hildesheim, *e.g.*, student-friendly pubs and bars in the city, and other social facilities. The group also got in contact with the International Office, to convince staff that the exchange community offered manifold advantages not only to incomings but also to the International Office itself, for example by lowering communication barriers to the target group as a whole. The exchange community is dependent on the nurturing of the community by members of the International Office or other permanent university structures. Only the future will tell whether the community has successfully established itself. Nevertheless, it creates a showcase that illustrates the potential of social information and communication software for knowledge management and informal learning.

To summarize, the concepts described and the ideas currently being developed and tested at the University of Hildesheim illustrate two possible ways to support intercultural exchange and learning through social information and communication tools. The results so far indicate, on the one hand, that from a *technical* perspective social information and communication infrastructures can be implemented with relative ease and little cost on the basis of open source software; on the other hand, seen from the *social* perspective, which is probably more important, success is mainly dependent on the activities of the facilitators and the involvement of the users.

Future Directions and Final Thoughts

THIS ESSAY HAS attempted to show the multitude of possibilities for employing ICT in the field of intercultural exchange and learning. The results from the projects described suggest that the use of information and communication technology can be seen as a worthwhile endeavor in this field. Current trends towards a participative social web seem not only to imply further advantages in using ICT in formal learning scenarios, but that they also have potential for fostering informal learning by providing free structures for self-initiated knowledge sharing and potentially unrestricted many-to-many communication. This paradigm shift in communication can be welcomed as a broadening of horizons in intercultural learning and exchange—Shirky's comment that the web empowers users to "organize without organizations" has already been quoted. Yet a look at the current situation in this area revealed a much narrower perspective, with most authors seeing social media as just another line of learning tools adoptable in "classroom" scenarios. Even initiatives with a wider scope are developed within existing institutional contexts, usually started and managed by traditional gatekeepers. So with regard to the potential of the social web it may be said that the future has not really started yet.

Apart from the line of argument that "encountering of the other" can be facilitated with the help of ICT, one should not forget that the notion of interculturality itself is not so clear in online environments and virtual settings. For example, Kern et al. (2004) see the internet "as an authentic communication medium in its own right" (254). Fostering language learning by bringing dislocated native and non-native speakers together seems to be a plausible and worthwhile undertaking. But one should be more cautious with similar expectations with respect to intercultural learning exchange. We started out from the idea that culture is something that is learned, cultivated within and shared by a group of people. Computer-mediated communication itself can have many effects on human behavior. The social presence of oneself or others is often restricted or limited. Social clues like age, ethnicity or gender are partly filtered out, especially in communication channels that are limited to written text. The possible effects are manifold and at least partly inconsistent, dependent not only on the technology but also reliant on individual behavior (individual preferences and competencies) and social online "culture" or norms. For example, hierarchies that are obvious in face-to-face situations, such as social rank based on professional position, seniority or gender, are often invisible or weakened in online settings. People may be uninhibited and yet still polite and helpful or, alternatively, they may behave with unexpected ruthlessness and aggressiveness. Users have a greater degree of control in the matter of self-presentation or building up an identity but less knowledge about the identity of others. Indeed, "on the internet nobody knows you're a dog" (*Wikipedia*). Some authors even speak of internet culture(s) (Bell 2001). So even if one rejects the view that the social web will transform human society as a whole, it is obvious that the concept of culture cannot be transferred on a one to one basis to online (communication) spaces. It is influenced, in fact, by many of the particularities that take effect in computer-mediated communication. Thus it may be modified, not be salient or not even visible at all in online communication (Hewling 2005, Ess / Sudweeks 2005). On the other hand, technology is not independent of culture (St. Amant 2002). Both concepts mutually influence each other. We may therefore conclude that ICT should only be used as a supplementary and not as the only tool for intercultural learning and exchange. At the same time, the emergence of a social web emphasizes the necessity for research on the effects of computer-mediated communication on the concept of interculturality itself.

References

Aoki, Kumiko / Kimura, Mary. "Telecollaboration 2.0: Using Facebook for Intercultural Exchange". In: *Proceedings of the World Conference on Educational Multimedia, Hypermedia and Telecommunications*. Ed. G. Siemens / C. Fulford. Chesapeake, VA: AACE, 2009, 135-44.

Baumgartner, Peter. "Web 2.0: Social Software & E-Learning." In: *Computer + Personal (CoPers), Special Issue: E-Learning und Social Software*, 34, 8, 2006, 20-22, 34.

Bell, David. *An Introduction to Cyberculture*. London: Routledge, 2001.

Bosse, Elke. "Intercultural Training and Development at Hildesheim University, Germany." In: *Intercultural Education*, 20, 5, 2009, 485–89.

Chan, Anthony / Frydenberg, Mark / Lee, Mark. "Facilitating Cross-cultural Learning through Collaborative Skypecasting." In: *Proceedings of the 8th ACM SIGITE Conference on Information Technology (Destin, FL, 2007)*, 59-66.

Dahl, Stephan. "Intercultural Research: The Current State of Knowledge" (Middlesex University Discussion Paper 26, 2004). In: *Social Science Research Network*. Website, <http://

papers.ssrn.com/sol3/papers.cfm?abstract_id=658202>

Davis, Boyd / Thiede, Ralf. "Writing into Change: Style Shifting in Asynchronous Electronic Discourse." In: *Network-based Language Teaching: Concepts and Practice*. Ed. Mark Warschauer / Richard Kern. Cambridge: Cambridge University Press, 2000, 87-120.

Dervin, Fred. *The Living Web (2.0) & Intercultural Education in Language Learning and Teaching (LLT)*. Website, <http://users.utu.fi/freder/sukol_2010.pdf>

Downes, Stephen. "E-Learning 2.0." In: *eLearn Magazine*, October 16th, 2005. Website, <http://elearnmag.org/subpage.cfm?section=articles&article=29-1>

Ess, Charles / Sudweeks, Fey. "Culture and Computer-mediated Communication: Toward New Understandings." In: *Journal of Computer-Mediated Communication*, 11, 1, 2005. Website, <http://jcmc.indiana.edu/vol11/issue1/ess.html>

Griesbaum, Joachim / Kepp, Saskia-Janina. "Facilitating Collaborative Knowledge Management and Self-directed Learning in Higher Education with the Help of Social Software: Concept and Implementation of CollabUni—a Social Information and Communication Infrastructure." In: *Proceedings of I-KNOW 2010 (10th International Conference on Knowledge Management and Knowledge Technologies, Graz, Austria, September 1st–3rd, 2010)*. Ed. Klaus Tochtermann / Hermann Maurer, 415-26.

Hewling, Anne. "Culture in the Online Class: Using Message Analysis to Look beyond Nationality-based Frames of Reference." In: *Journal of Computer-Mediated Communication*, 11, 1, 2005. Website, <http://jcmc.indiana.edu/vol11/issue1/hewling.html>

Kahiigi, Evelyn Kigozi / Ekenberg, Love / Hansson, Henrik / Tusubira, F. F. / Danielson, Mats. "Exploring the E-Learning State of Art." In: *EJEL*, 6, 2, 2008, 77-88.

Kern, Richard / Ware, Paige / Warschauer, Mark. "Crossing Frontiers: New Directions in Online Pedagogy and Research." In: *Annual Review of Applied Linguistics*, 24, 2004, 243-60.

Krishna, S. / Sahay, Sundeep / Walsham, Geoff. "Managing Cross-Cultural Issues in Global Software Outsourcing." In: *Communications of the ACM (Association for Computing Machinery)*, 47, 4, 2004, 62-66.

Law, Effie Lai-chong / Nguyen-ngoc, Anh Vu / Kuru, Selahattin. "Mixed-Method Validation of Pedagogical Concepts for an Intercultural Online Learning Environment: A Case Study." In: *Proceedings of the 2007 International ACM Conference on Supporting Group Work (Sanibel Island, FL)*, 321-30.

Lee, Lina. "Learners' Perspectives on Networked Collaborative Interaction with Native Speakers of Spanish in the US." In: *Language Learning and Technology*, 8, 1, 2004, 83-100.

O'Dowd, Robert. "Evaluating the outcomes of online intercultural exchange." In: *ELT Journal*, 61, 2, 2007a, 144-52.

------------ (Ed). *Online Intercultural Exchange: An Introduction for Foreign Language Teachers*. Clevedon, Somerset: Multilingual Matters, 2007b.

"On the Internet, nobody knows you're a dog." In: *Wikipedia*. Website, <http://en.wikipedia.org/wiki/On_the_Internet,_nobody_knows_you're_a_dog>

O'Reilly, Tim. *What is Web 2.0?: Design Patterns and Business Models for the Next Generation of Software*, September 30th, 2005. Website, <http://www.oreilly.de/artikel/web20.html>

Prensky, Marc. "Digital Natives, Digital Immigrants." In: *On the Horizon* (Bradford, West Yorks.: MCB University Press), 9, 5, 2001, 1-6.

Ritchie, Mathy. *Intercultural Computer-Mediated Communication Exchange and the Development of Sociolinguistic Competence*. Doctoral thesis, University of Victoria, Canada, 2009. Also as a website, <http://dspace.library.uvic.ca:8080/bitstream/1828/1368/1/Dissertation.MRitchie.Avril09.pdf>

St. Amant, Kirk. "When Cultures and Computers Collide:

Rethinking Computer-Mediated Communication according to International and Intercultural Communication Expectations." In: *Journal of Business and Technical Communication*, 16, 2, 2002, 196-214.

Samovar, Larry A. / Porter, Richard E. / McDaniel, Edwin R. *Communication between Cultures*. Seventh edition. Boston, MA: Wadsworth, 2010.

Savignon, Sandra J. / Rothmeier, Waltraud. "Computer-mediated Communication: Texts and Strategies." In: *CALICO Journal*, 21, 2, 2004, 265-90.

Shirky, Clark. *Here Comes Everybody: The Power of Organizing without Organizations*. Harmondsworth, Middx.: Penguin Books, 2008.

Vygotsky, Lev S. *Mind in Society: The Development of Higher Psychological Processes*. Cambridge, MA: Harvard University Press, 1979.

ENCOUNTERING OTHERS ONLINE

by THOMAS MANDL

PEOPLE SPEND A good amount of time in front of computers today and even use them while walking around. Moreover, meeting other people is an activity which has now been partially moved to the virtual world. Social networks are not only created in real space but also in so-called social software systems like Facebook, StudiVZ, MySpace or Orkut.

These social software systems are powerful tools for human communication and interaction. Social software networks have become popular around the world. Facebook claims to have half a million users worldwide (Wauters 2010). Users communicate, exchange information objects such as photographs, organize their existing acquaintances and find new contacts. When searching for information on others, 48 per cent of internet users rely on such network systems according to a recent survey (Madden / Smith 2010). Especially among young internet users, these social software systems are highly popular and markets have been growing steadily. We extend the analysis to blogs, the online diaries which have also become quite popular in recent years. Because of their ease of use and facility to connect people by means of the comments and links, we also consider them as social software. Moreover, great expectations are projected for blogs in connection with information management in companies. The research on blogs has many similarities to the analysis of social networks (Agarwal / Liu 2008).

Using the above-mentioned systems, anyone can have friends anywhere in the world and interact with them. Virtual networks seem to be of universal appeal and are being used on a global level. These systems seem to be a great leap forward in facilitating international exchange. May they soon help to overcome the problems of intercultural communication? Are they the technological tool which can foster understanding around the world? Has globalization through information technology already achieved a major goal?

Things are not as easy as they seem to be. There is considerable empirical evidence that these social network systems often cannot be easily accessed for international interaction and therefore for meeting people in other countries. In this paper, we intend to first take a closer look at some of these systems and then compare them to each other. It will be seen that, despite their family similarities, social network systems are indeed very different across cultures. Users of social networks Mostly make online friends and those who live close to them. A study of Facebook users also showed that virtual friends are often not very distant physically (Thelwall 2009).

This homophily of online friendship has been described, *e.g.*, by Thom-Santelli *et al.* (2010), who analyzed 400,000 connections among IBM employees in their internal social network site. It turned out that the large majority of the links are to people within the same country. Interestingly, and unlike most other network systems, links in the IBM network are not reciprocal. This may be due to the internal need to model hierarchical structures. The homophily observed in social networks is analogous to the link structure of the internet. Most links go to sites within the same country (Thelwall 2004). Not only language can explain this observation—culture seems to be an important factor as well.

Culture as observed human behavior has a great impact on the development and use of information technology. Virtual chats are a good example of a situation where cultural habits and values need to adapt to a new environment. In real face-to-face communication, standards and conventions are well established to signal that one partner may want to end the communication. For virtual chats, these signals are not yet fully established. This can led to some uncomfortable and unclear situations for many users from cultures with a high emphasis on politeness.

When people work with a computer or use it in their spare time, they are confronted with the human-computer interface. Currently, user interfaces are for the most part visual, so they are basically everything that we see on a screen. Comparing interfaces across different cultures shows that these technological artefacts are often notably different. Asian interfaces may look burdened and overcrowded to a Western user, whereas Chinese may find Western interfaces boring and empty. The information density expected and preferred is one of the obvious differences (Heimgärtner 2005, Würtz 2004).

There are good reasons for designing items differently. Expectations with regard to visual design are deeply rooted in culture. Interfaces on computer screens are perceived differently by people from around the world. An experiment with the well-known and quite sober interface of the Google web search engine has shown that to be true. An eye tracking study revealed that users scan different areas and their attention is directed to different parts of the screen. German test users focused more on the top elements. On the other hand, Japanese participants scanned more areas that were further down the page (Duda *et al.* 2008). This is evidence for a more holistic perception of user interfaces in the Eastern cultures. Chinese search engine users tend to click on result pages lower down in the ranked list than Western Google users.

A closer look at social networks in different countries shows that a similar market situation has emerged in most developed countries. It is striking that in most countries one or two market leaders have achieved a dominant market position (ComScore 2007, Callari n.d.). Exporting a social software system to another country hardly ever leads to a significant market share.

This seems to be due to the cultural issues involved in social media. Since these networks are created to support people in their social lives and organize their social contacts in the online world, these systems need to be heavily adapted to the way in which social life is organized in a particular culture. It seems that the local market leader can adapt much better to such cultural needs than foreign competitors.

It would be advisable to identify the particularities of the market leaders in order to gain insights into the differences between social software in a variety of cultures. The market leaders are, for example, Xing (www.xing.com) and studiVZ (www.studivz.net) in Germany, Vkontakte.ru and Odnoklassniki.ru in Russia, QQ (www.qq.com) in China, Mixi (mixi.jp) in Japan, Orkut (www.orkut.com) in Brazil and India, Facebook (www.facebook.com) and MySpace (www.myspace.com) in the USA, Friendster and Imeem in the Philippines and Islam Net in the Arab Countries (www.muxlim.com).

Especially in collectivist countries like Korea and China, social network systems were founded early on and have achieved considerable success. Cyworld in Korea has been active since 1999 and QQ in China even since 1997. In absolute numbers, there are more users of social networks in the USA than in other countries. Over 140 million US users compared, for example, to 47 million Japanese, 30 million in Brazil, and 18 million in Italy, according to a study in December 2009 (The Nielsen Company 2010). However, this is due to differences in the technological infrastructure and the wealth of countries. According to another study, thirty per cent of the entire population in South Korea have an account on Cyworld and more than half of the internet users have logged in within the last month, whereas in the USA fewer than twenty-five per cent have done so (Anderson 2007). It seems that collectivist countries are more attracted by social networking services. A survey by the media company Universal McCann revealed that the Philippines, Mexico, India and Pakistan use social networks most and find blogs useful for socializing. All these countries are ranked relatively low on Hofstede's Individualism Index (IDV), with Pakistan being extremely low. Some of the other countries with high collectivism scores are not very technologically developed and, as a consequence, were not included in the survey.

The visual design and appearance of Asian social media applications is different from Western social media sites just as for other web sites—as discussed above. A study on navigation, metaphors, mental models and the appearance of social networks has been carried out for Korea, Japan and the USA (Marcus / Krishnamurthi 2009). There are more graphic elements and more functions related to visual information like pictures and videos in the Asian systems than in Western systems. This can be explained by the high context communication style which relies not merely on explicit verbal information. Both facilitate the visual display of the current emotion of the user. Entertainment plays a more important role. QQ includes transmissions of live shows. The emphasis is on the community and less on the presentation of the individual person. QQ and Cyworld have very successful business models which fit the cultures very well. The companies generate revenue from the sale of digital goods, *e.g.*, background music, avatars, and small objects for individual homepages or casual games (Plus Eight Star 2006; Tencent 2009). In Cyworld, a large portion of the objects are bought as presents for others. This digital goods culture supports the elaborate gift-giving culture in Korea which is typical of a collectivist culture.

An ongoing international comparison between social network services analyzed Turkish, Indian and German network systems. It turned out that Turkish sites rely more on graphic design and offer more design options regarding color and fonts to their members (for them to modify their individual pages) than German sites do.

Asian network sites have their particularities, which Western users might not easily understand. The Korean Cyworld has an elaborate system with *degrees of friendship*. These are translations of degrees of blood-relationships in the real world. This shows that in-groups are systematically organized into several layers of friends. Such layers are not so common in Western countries and this shows how an extremely collectivist society needs to define more elaborately what a friend and a group are. It is necessary due to the consequences of membership of a group which requires a high degree of loyalty. Cyworld also allows the creation of a mini-room in pseudo-3D on the homepage of the users. This feature serves the demand for space in a densely populated country and opens up opportunities for the gift culture, again typical of a collectivist society like South Korea.

Like many Western systems, the Japanese service Mixi does not allow immediate access to the profiles of other users. It is not meant for finding new friends, but rather for staying in contact with friends or communities. This can be explained in terms of the long-term orientation and collectivist nature of Japanese culture. Safety and trust within the in-group are emphasized. The extension of the social network is based mainly on invitations. Facebook, on the other hand, allows its members to find new friends more easily, as you would expect from a more individualistic and short-term oriented culture in which new relationships are established more frequently. Facebook allows users to use their real names. Combined with the low restrictions on access to the profiles, it is obvious that Facebook or MySpace are more oriented toward the self-presentation that is typical of an individualistic society (Toto 2008).

The types of online activities that are popular also differ among societies. Koreans and Chinese seem to be more active and to read and write blogs, whereas those in more individualistic societies like France, Germany, the United Kingdom and the USA read and write blogs less frequently than the global average (Universal McCann 2008). For uploading videos, the three big East Asian societies are well above global average and China is well ahead in video consumption (Universal McCann 2008). Online video consumption is also very popular in Brazil and Mexico. Not for all these phenomena can an explanation based on cultural dimensions easily be found. They need to be understood as a complex interplay of cultural, personal, economic and political factors.

Also, blog systems differ very considerably, as noted by Park *et al.* (2006). A manual analysis of 700 blog pages including the comments and reactions attached to them revealed culturally diverse patterns. The study showed that the virtue of "keeping face" is very important for Chinese and has an impact on the discussion and communication patterns. There are less negative reactions in the Chinese set. A more detailed look at the negative reactions shows that they usually contain more text than negative reactions in the contrasting German set. If Chinese do react negatively, they feel a greater need to elaborate the reasons for that (Mandl 2009).

An interesting quantitative study on the frequency of opinion expressions in news texts shows that there are significant differences in the frequency of expression of subjectivity and their polarity. The subjectivity and polarity differ across a corpus of news extracted from the web in nine languages (Bautin *et al.* 2008). As would be expected, a negative statement in one language is not necessarily equivalent to a negative statement in another language. But would all users be aware of that?

Social networks and blogs are not universal tools. Certainly they are applied in very different ways as tools. Their application is bound to the needs and the characteristics of a culture. Just entering a network or installing one in an international enterprise without any awareness of cultural differences is not a promising approach. Systems from other cultures may seem disturbingly different to users. They are strangers on the internet, just as people from other countries are.

References

Agarwal, Nitin / Liu, Huan. "Blogosphere: Research Issues, Tools, and Applications." In: *SIGKDD Explorations Newsletter*, 10, 1, 2008, 18-31.

Anderson, Nate. "Report: South Korea Tops in Social Networking, US Fifth." In: *ars technica*, July 9th, 2007. Website, <http://arstechnica.com/old/content/2007/07/report-south-korea-tops-in-social-network-us-fifth.ars>

Bautin, Mikhail / Vijayarenu, Lohit / Skiena, Steven. "International Sentiment Analysis for News and Blogs." In: *Proceedings of the Second International Conference on Weblogs and Social Media (ICWSM-2008), Seattle, WA, March 30th-April 2nd, 2008*. Ed. Eytan Adar *et al*. Menlo Park, CA: The AAAI Press, 2008, 19-26.

Callari, Ron. "Top Ten Social Networks Circumnavigating the Globe." In: *InventorSpot*. Website, <http://inventorspot.com/articles/top_ten_social_networks_circumnavigating_globe_30018>

ComScore. "Press Release: Social Networking Goes Global." In: *Comscore*, July 31st, 2007. Website, <http://comscore.com/Press_Events/Press_Releases/2007/07/Social_Networking_Goes_Global>

Duda, Sabrina / Schiessl, Michael / Nüsperling, Stefan. "See the World with Diffferent Eyes." In: *planung & analyse market research*, 2008, 14-18.

Heimgärtner, Rüdiger. "Messen von kulturellen Unter-schieden in der Mensch-Computer-Interaktion." In: *Workshop-Proceedings der 5. fachübergreifenden Konferenz Mensch und Computer, September 4th-7th, 2005, Linz, Österreich*, 89-92.

Hofstede, Geert / Hofstede, Gert Jan. *Cultures and Organizations: Software of the Mind* (1991). Second edition. New York: McGraw-Hill, 2005.

Madden, Mary / Smith, Aaron. "Reputation Management and Social Media." In: *PewInternet*, May 26th, 2010. Website, <http://pewinternet.org/Reports/2010/Reputation-Management.aspx>

Mandl, Thomas. "Comparing Chinese and German Blogs." In: *Twentieth ACM Conference on Hypertext and Hypermedia (HT '09), Torino, June 29th-July 1st, 2009*. New York: ACM Press, 299-308.

Marcus, Aaron / Krishnamurthi, Niranjan. "Cross-cultural Analysis of Social Network Services in Japan, Korea, and the USA." In: *Internationalization, Design and Global Development, Proceedings of the Third International Conference (IDGD 2009). San Diego, July 19th-24th, 2009.* San Diego, CA: HCI International, 2009, 59-68.

Nielsen Company, The. "Led by Facebook, Twitter, Global Time Spent on Social Media Sites up 82% Year over Year." In: *Nielsenwire*, January 22nd, 2010. Website, <http://blog.nielsen.com/nielsenwire/global/led-by-facebook-twitter-global-time-spent-on-social-media-sites-up-82-year-over-year/>

Park, S. Joon / Zhang, Qiping / Ma, Shanshan. "A Comparative Study on Public-hosted Blog Sites in the US, China, and Korea." In: *Proceedings of the American Society for Information Science and Technology (ASIST)*, 43, 1, 2006, 1-12.

Plus Eight Star. *Inside Cyworld: Best Practices from inside South Korea's Leading Online Community* (2006). Website, <http://www.plus8star.com/Inside_Cyworld_Sample.pdf>

Tencent. *Tencent Report 2009: US $ 1 Billion Can't Be Wrong!* Website, <http://www.plus8star.com/2009/08/13/inside-tencent-report-2009-us1-billion-cant-be-wrong/>

Thelwall, Mike. *Link analysis: An Information Science Approach.* San Diego, CA: Academic Press, 2004.

------------. "Homophily in MySpace." In: *Journal of the American Society for Information Science and Technology (ASIST)*, 60, 2, 2009, 219-31.

Thom-Santelli, Jennifer / Millen, David R. / DiMicco, Joan M. "Characterizing Global Participation in an Enterprise SNS." In: *International Conference on Intercultural Collaboration (ICIC), August 19th-20th, 2010, Copenhagen, Denmark.*

Toto, Serkan. "Taking Social Networks Abroad: Why MySpace and Facebook Are Failing in Japan." In: *TechCrunch*, August 3rd, 2008. Website, <http://techcrunch.com/2008/08/03/taking-social-networks-abroad-why-myspace-and-facebook-are-failing-in-japan/>

Universal McCann. *When Did We Start Trusting Strangers?:*

How the Internet Turned Us All into Influencers. Report, September 2008. Website, <http://www.imaginar.org/docs/when_did_we_start_trusting_strangers.pdf>

Wauters, Robin. "Zuckerberg Makes It Official: Facebook Hits 500 Million Members." In: *TechCrunch*, July 21st, 2010. Website, <http://techcrunch.com/2010/07/21/facebook-500-million/>

Würtz, Elisabeth. "Intercultural Communication on Websites: An Analysis of Visual Communication of High- and Low-context Cultures." In: *Proceedings of the Fourth International Conference on Cultural Attitudes towards Technology and Communication (CATAC), 2004, Murdoch University, Western Australia,* 109-22.

SELF-EXPRESSION IN ONLINE NETWORKS

AN INTERCULTURAL COMPARISON

by Maria Möstl, Christa Womser-Hacker & Joachim Griesbaum

WHEN THE INTERNET changed from a medium of scientific exchange to a mass medium in the mid-Nineties, the impact that it would have on society was unpredictable. The development towards a mass medium, which has had such a huge influence on today's communication forms and information behavior, happened very fast—measured by the recent pace of technical development. Within a few years daily use of the internet became routine, and it became a permanent part of people's everyday lives. The users themselves shape the virtual space to a great extent by creating and sharing content with other users. To stand out in this globally networked, virtual world, it is a challenge for users to present themselves as *interesting* to others.

By now self-expression on the internet has become a natural part of media activity for many young people. The internet offers people many different possibilities to express and present themselves through media. Online networks in particular enjoy great popularity. Social online networks enable their users not only to communicate with others, but also provide them with a chance to present themselves. They do so by sharing their privacy with others.

Not for a long time now has *private* been understood as the opposite of *public*. Privacy instead stands for the self-determined handling of personal information. People can decide for themselves what others can learn about them, and the following premise apparently applies: *Those who reveal a lot about themselves become interesting.* The insufficient protection of one's privacy is however an underestimated issue, which has often been ignored due to the complicated and tedious business of privacy settings.

This article discusses the roles that privacy and self-expression today play in the use of social online networks. It investigates to what extent the concepts influence each other and whether there are cultural differences in the use of social online networks in relation to privacy protection and self-expression. For this purpose a survey of German and American Facebook users was conducted with the help of an online questionnaire. The aim was to obtain insights into the perception of privacy and self-expression behavior of German and American social online network users.

Social Networks

MITCHELL (1969) DESCRIBES social networks as "a specific set of linkages among a defined set of persons, with the additional property that the characteristics of these linkages as a whole may be used to interpret the social behavior of the persons involved" (2).

According to that there are three important criteria that might be used for the characterization of a network: the structure of the network, meaning its size and density; the goals and functions, meaning what the parties want; and the quality of the relations between the persons. Especially this last factor plays a crucial part in characterizing a network, since there are many different forms, like weak relations, work-related relations or family relations.

boyd [*sic*] / Ellison (2007) give an overview of social networking sites and social online networks. Such networks can be described as web-based communities that are usually characterized by a combination of the following functions and components:

Personal profile with different possibilities of privacy setting

Friend/contact list or address book with management settings

Receiving and sending messages from/to other members

Receiving and sending of system-generated notifications about different events (profile changes, uploaded pictures/videos, links, contact requests)

Search

SixDegrees.com was the first website that connected personal profiles with lists of friends. It can be seen as the ancestor of present day online social networks and was online from 1997 till 2000. In 2002 the social network boom started with the launch of Friendster, and continued with platforms like MySpace (launched 2003), Hi5 (2003), Facebook (2004), Bebo (2005), StudiVZ (2005) and others. Today Facebook alone—the most popular social online network—consists of more than 500 million user profiles. The attractiveness of these networks may be traced back to the various fields of application like the option to get in contact with people that one couldn't get to know by offline means or to find old friends again. Social networks offer more versatile communication channels than email, telephone or face-to-face encounters alone. They also provide many possibilities for communicating information about your personality or even for forming and displaying your Self.

Self and Self-Expression in Social Networks

THE SELF IS not so much a concrete definition of a person and his or her personality as an abstract view of the whole person, especially the cognitive processes whose subject that person is (Schachinger 2002, 26). Depending on the situation and the environment, one can call upon different self-images. Conversely, this means that every person possesses not only a stable Core-Self but also an adjustable Role-Self that is responsible for situational appropriateness, dynamics and modification.

Self-expression describes the kind of behavior towards others or society in general that a person displays in order to control or influence the perception that others have of that person's character. The subject that is displayed and presented is the Self, though a different kind of behavior will be displayed depending on the particular situation and audience. Usually there are certain self-interested goals that are pursued by the use of this behavior, such as making a positive impression on others or gaining their appreciation. Strictly speaking, the person who underlies this could be described as misleading and deluding, but self-expression does not have to be conscious or purposeful behavior. A certain self-presentation can be triggered unconsciously or as a matter of routine.

Also, the desire to be acknowledged and liked leads to people trying to present themselves in a preferably convenient but not necessarily fitting way. Self-expression takes place constantly and can also be directed at oneself. The image that people have of themselves results to a great extent from the images that *others* have of them, or rather from the images that they *assume*—from the reactions—that they have. Self-expression therefore has repercussions on self-image.

The image that people communicate in real life is not consistent or fully self-determined. A person may try to form his own Self according to his own wishes, but this will always be influenced by others. Many people have many different images of the same person. These different images will likewise evoke different adjustment reactions from this person, which will again affect their self-concept and therefore even, though to a different extent, their Self. The variety of public images and especially their diversity lead to contradictory self-images. Images that you compile about other people are closely related to your own self-images. Other people are evaluated by reference to your own key attributes. These can be attributes that you value very much, or the contrary.

A permanent switching between perspectives is necessary for a Self that is adjusted to the environment. But occasionally it can be very stressful to have to adjust the Self to people and situations, and maintaining credibility can be especially hard when you are behaving inconsistently.

It would be much easier to create the Self to one's own standards and wishes and to present it like that. The web and social online networks in particular open a new and convenient space for self-expression. There are many ways to influence the impression that others obtain of you—for example, by only sharing pictures that you like, or by posting hobbies, *etc.*, that are likely to make a good impression on others. The general configuration and design of a profile alone can evoke a specific image of a person. However, the authenticity of such an image is much harder to check than in real life. One may tend to give credit to this first impression. Without a doubt social networks can be described as platforms for self-expression. But there are differences: motives, extent and means are as diverse as the members. And the kind of network (its purpose and the context of its use) has an influence on the extent of self-expression.

State of Research

WITH THE GROWING number of users of social online networks and the consequent discussions on data protection, research is focusing more and more on the phenomenon of social networks. A variety of studies have analyzed the behavior of users, their motivations, their concerns about privacy on the Internet and the resulting changes in their behavior with regard to the disclosure of their personal data.

These studies show clearly that many users reveal personal information to a great extent. One of the main explanations for this behavior is that many members think that a certain degree of disclosure is necessary to make a social network useful at all (Gross / Acquisti 2005, 75). Young / Quan-Haase (2009) found in their study that about two-thirds of the participants revealed their sexual orientation, their relationship status and interests (268). Strater / Richter Lipford (2008) also found out that users are often not aware of what information they are actually providing in their profile (114). According to Young / Quan-Haase, earlier studies already showed that users with a larger social network are more open and communicate more of their personal data, as well as users with relatively little concern about the security of data on the web.

Empirical Study

THE CENTRAL GOAL of this study was to investigate the question of privacy and data protection in social online networks on an intercultural level, to which end an online survey was conducted. The research aim focused on the following questions.

How important is the protection of privacy when using social online networks?

Does the need for positive self-expression influence the handling of security and privacy?

Are there cultural differences in the use of Facebook in terms of privacy and security?

Does self-assessment of one's own data protection be-
haviour match with reality?

Are there significant age differences in the use of online social networks and in dealing with privacy and
security?

The population for this study was defined as all German and
US users who were registered on Facebook before their participation in the online survey. The links to the online surveys were
distributed through various forums, Facebook groups and mail-
ing lists. In the four weeks of the survey period a total of 462
subjects participated in two surveys, of whom 340 participants
finished the survey and 122 dropped out early.

The questionnaire includes 26 items, which are grouped into
the categories *demographic data*, *usage patterns*, *privacy and
security*, and *self-expression*.

Results

THE SURVEY RESULTS show that the subjects seldom focus primarily
on protecting their privacy in their usage patterns. The privacy
settings are varied less often than the profile content is, and the
knowledge of the exact settings is much less accurate than the
knowledge of the profile information. Apparently the actual
profile has a higher priority in the overall context of network
usage than the protection of the profile content itself.

Nearly fifty per cent of the users surveyed are friends with
at least a hundred people or more in the network. Only eight
per cent have customized settings when it comes to restricting
access to their own data for other users. The label "friends"
tempts users to classify these people as reliable, without
worrying sufficiently about whether in a face-to-face meeting
with these people they would entrust them with their information without further concern. Taking into account the fact
that eighty per cent of the respondents are in regular offline

contact with less than fifty per cent of their online friends, the "quality-gap" or difference between offline and online friends becomes obvious. When users *do* try to protect themselves, they do it especially on sensitive issues such as personal photos and contact details—a certain degree of sensitivity regarding the protection of personal data is therefore there. Looking at the relationship between the quantity of the information presented and the overall attractiveness assessment, it is clear that their own sense of attractiveness is positively influenced by the number of profile items. This selective self-presentation also affects the handling of data and security protection to a certain negative degree. The need to appear positively in the eyes of others weighs much heavier than the potential risks of negative consequences caused by too much openness or by data abuse.

Comparing the German to the US users, some differences were noted. (Due to the different lengths of time since the establishment of the network in the two countries, there are for example variations in the length of membership, number of friends or amount of shared information.) When it comes to log-in and changing the profile content, frequency results indicate that American users use Facebook with more intensity. This prolonged use is probably due to the greater confidence in the safety of the platform on the part of Americans. Results also indicate that German participants use the platform less for self-expression than the Americans do. But since nearly ninety per cent of the German participants think that others present themselves on Facebook in a better light than they are in real life, the concept of self-staging does not seem to be completely unfamiliar to them. This assumption, however, requires further empirical verification.

When comparing different age groups, the results illustrate that there is no relevant difference in general usage patterns between them. Age also seems not to have any influence on the network size of the participants. Nevertheless, the study shows that on average younger members are registered for a longer time period than older members, implying that older members did not "grow" with the social network and therefore did not have more time to adapt to it. Comparing the amount of shared information, it is clear that younger members share much more than the older ones. Therefore younger users can be judged as somewhat more communicative, but they do not use more or stronger data protecting options. This implies that younger users are somewhat more careless with data protection.

Interestingly, some participants noted at the end of the survey that they had only become aware of their current privacy settings through the survey—and therefore changed them afterwards to meet their personal needs. Another interesting point is that some participants mentioned that anybody who uses Facebook knows that they are "selling their soul to the Facebook company". Therefore it would be pointless to adjust anything in the privacy settings! A better option would be to post only stuff that you can take responsibility for. Information that you don't want the whole world to know shouldn't be posted in the first place. If all users acted according to this premise, there would be much less sensitive data on the web that could be abused or sold or could harm the users in any other way. On the other hand, the online networks would lose a lot of their popularity, because they actually live on what their members produce.

Résumé

SOCIAL NETWORKING SITES enable and enhance possibilities of communication as well as the initiation and maintainance of friendships and acquaintances. The motive of "maintaining contacts" is the reason most often given for using social networks. On social online networks one can follow the lives of friends, family and acquaintances, and also keep them updated with relatively little effort. Social online networks clearly satisfy the human need to be close to others. But many users are not aware of or repress the negative consequences that come with this. It seems that the advantages of these networks far outweigh the perceived dangers and possible risks.

The findings of the study show a correlation between self-expression and the handling of privacy. The more intensely a user employs Facebook as a tool to create an attractive profile, the greater the probability that he will neglect his privacy protection. Nevertheless, users seem to possess a certain degree of awareness with respect to the sensitivity of provided or generated online information. In international comparison, the results show that US users seems to be less suspicious in dealing with the network and therefore interact more with it by updating their profile more often and by sharing more information. Concepts of friendship differ for cultural reasons, and on average Germans have fewer friends than Americans (Kalberg 2000, 132). Most of the US users do not distinguish between their friends, and they grant the same level of access to all online friends (contacts) equally. American users not only share more information in general, they also make it accessible to a bigger circle. This can be explained in terms of their greater trust in Facebook. As online social networks become ubiquitous and are integrated more and more into people's personal and maybe even professional lives, one could argue that this investigation has only scratched the surface of a new development in communication.

Private information (*i.e.*, information directly addressed to certain people only) is increasingly being offered in commercial spaces of publicly available information (*i.e.*, information easily accessed by large numbers of people). Encountering the Other, seen as the unknown recipient of personal information, seems to be an area in which some cultures appear to be more comfortable than others.

References

boyd, danah m. [*sic*] / Ellison, Nicole B. "Social Network Sites: Definition, History, and Scholarship." In: *Journal of Computer-mediated Communication*, 13, 1, Article 11, 2007.

Website, <http://jcmc.indiana.edu/vol13/issue1/boyd.ellison. html>

Facebook—Statistics, 2010. Website, <http://www.facebook. com/press/info.php?statistics>

Gross, Ralph / Acquisti, Alessandro. "Information Revelation and Privacy in Online Social Networks." In: *WEPS '05: Proceedings of the 2005 ACM Workshop on Privacy in the Electronic Society. Alexandria, VA, 2005,* 71-80.

Kalberg, Stephen. "Formen der Interaktion von Akademikern: Eine Ebene des strukturierten Missverständnisses." In: *Die Vermessung kultureller Unterschiede: USA und Deutschland im Vergleich.* Ed. Jürgen Gerhards. Opladen: Westdeutscher Verlag, 2000, 127-39.

Mitchell, J. Clyde. "The Concept and Use of Social Networks." In: *Social Networks in Urban Situations: Analysis of Personal Relationships in Central African Towns.* Ed. J. Clyde Mitchell. Manchester: Manchester University Press, 1969, 1-50.

Schachinger, Helga. *Das Selbst, die Selbsterkenntnis und das Gefühl für den eigenen Wert.* Bern: Huber, 2002.

Strater, Katherine / Richter Lipford, Heather. "Strategies and Struggles with Privacy in an Online Social Networking Community." In: *Proceedings of the 22nd British HCI Group Annual Conference on People and Computers: Culture, Creativity, Interaction—Volume 1. Liverpool, 2008,* 111-19.

Young, Alyson L. / Quan-Haase, Anabel. "Information Revelation and Internet Privacy Concerns on Social Network Sites: A Case Study of Facebook." In: *C & T '09: Proceedings of the Fourth International Conference on Communities and Technologies. University Park, PA, 2009,* 265-74.

THE HILDESHEIM INTERCULTURAL FILM DATABASE

by FRANCIS JARMAN

As WELL AS entertaining us, films (movies) often show inter-action between people from different cultures, and so they constitute an important resource for anyone who is interested in studying or teaching intercultural communication. This, despite the fact that the accuracy of film "reality" will always be open to question. Like literature, the movies imitate life, but they offer a *version* of it rather than aiming at an exact copy. (Nor are the products of documentary or news film-makers necessarily better in this respect, since all filming involves manipulation and intervention by the film-maker, whether in the choice of content, the timing, the lighting, the camera angles, or the cutting and editing of the film material.)

To us today, early efforts by movie-makers to portray the ethnic Other frequently seem ridiculous. In the golden age of the cinema, commercial movies probably got other cultures *wrong* far more often than they got them *right*. And yet who was to know? Very few people traveled, and in Europe the flood of immigrants from former colonies had not yet begun. There were brief movie newsreels, but television was in its infancy, there were no satellite broadcasts from distant continents, and certainly no internet.

If you wanted to portray Africans, you used Afro-American

actors. A few British or American actors of Asian origin or "exotic" appearance had the market for "orientals" pretty much cornered. And very often Caucasian actors were drafted in to play non-Caucasian parts, sometimes with ludicrous results. For the period before the Second World War, this kind of casting might, for common-sense reasons, be easier to excuse. With a few exceptions like the Indian child star Sabu, the studios had hardly any Asian "stars" on their books, and major roles as Asians tended to go to actors like Paul Muni and Luise Rainer (in *The Good Earth*), Peter Lorre ("Mr. Moto") and Sylvia Sidney ("Madame Butterfly"), who specialized in "exotic" roles. But this continued to happen as late as the Eighties, despite the availability of experienced, English-speaking actors from (for example) one of the world's greatest film industries, India. An APPENDIX to this essay lists, for instance, just a few of the Western actors who (since 1945) have played Asian or Eurasian roles.

Perhaps the nadir was reached with the casting of a wholesome Californian girl, Amy Irving, as the Indian princess Anjuli in the television film version of *The Far Pavilions* (1983), a disaster which prompted Salman Rushdie to note that Irving's make-up person obviously believed "that Indian princesses [dipped] their eyes in black ink and [got] sun-tans on their lips" (1984). Another British novelist, Julian Barnes (1986), commented that, in films of this kind, "a tenacious imperialism haunts the casting [...]. Promotion for real Indians stops at the rank of second-in-command; though they can, of course, play as many poor, unruly, violent and superstitious natives as they like".

There is now undoubtedly a greater commitment among film-makers to aim at ethnographic consistency and accuracy. Ethnic clichés will still be served up, but as "camp"—not to be taken seriously—in films like those of the James Bond and Indiana Jones series. This new emphasis on ethnographic plausibility may be partly for biographical reasons, as directors now increasingly have international careers, or for reasons of professional pride; it can also be attributed to the fact that modern audiences are more familiar with distant countries and cultures, and thus more critical when confronted with cheap, unconvincing clichés; but it is arguably also because film-makers have become more aware of the potential in an intercultural plot for showing conflict, lively interaction between film characters, and the poetry, magic and color of the unfamiliar. In other words—for good film-making.

The movies can highlight, focus, entertain and inspire us in ways that documentary films cannot. They invite viewers to get involved with the characters emotionally—and empathy is a prerequisite for understanding across the divide of cultural difference, and "a response that has been widely recognized as critical to successful cross-cultural interactions" (Summerfield 1993, 3). Although movies should not be mistaken for real life, they lead their audiences back to it, more thoughtful about the people and cultures that they have encountered.

Movies are a rich source of critical incidents. Excerpts that present clear examples of intercultural communication or conflict can be analyzed and evaluated, and this is what the individual contributions to the Hildesheim Intercultural Film Database (IcFilmDB) set out to do. The IcFilmDB evolved out of a project seminar for postgraduate students that began in summer 2005. The students (including visiting students from other countries who were in Hildesheim as participants in academic exchange programs like ERASMUS) present their findings in class and later upload their work onto a website that was set up and is still technically managed by Björn Quast, MA, a Hildesheim University graduate.

The excerpts are evaluated in terms of the attitudes or behavior broadly characteristic of members of particular cultures with regard to certain key areas of life—the so-called **cultural dimensions**. ("Culture" is understood to encompass ethnic minorities as well as the classic national cultures.) A catalog of twenty dimensions is used. This is based on the *Hildesheim Orientation Matrix* proposed by Beneke (2001) and expanded and slightly modified by Jarman (2006), the individual cultural dimensions being derived from the work of Talcott Parsons, Edward T. Hall, Geert Hofstede, Fons Trompenaars, Vern Terpstra, Ronald Inglehart, and other such authorities.

Since most of the dimensions can be represented as a continuum between two poles, comparisons between cultural positions are easily possible. In recognition of the complex and changing nature of cultural behavior patterns, no attempt is made to produce quantifications or indices in the way that (for example) Hofstede does. The dangers that are inherent in generalization are well-known, but the potential rewards of the approach adopted for the IcFilmDB far outweigh the risks. Several other methodologies were considered, but a culture-comparative focus was chosen—for reasons of efficiency and economy—in preference (for example) to alternatives based on detailed analysis of individual cultures (Alexander Thomas's "Culture Standards" approach) or those entailing a close, discourse-analytical reading of selected scenes.

THE TWENTY DIMENSIONS are as follows (with, in each case, a short illustrative example extracted from the analyses in the film database):

1. Individualism/Collectivism

In *Hsi-Yen* (*The Wedding Banquet*, dir. Ang Lee, USA 1993, analyzed by BENEDIKTA GRISSEMANN, ARIANE WILHUS and VY DO), Wai-Tung is living happily in New York, in a stable gay relationship with his partner Simon, when his parents in China decide that it is time for him to be married. First they hire a dating service to find him a suitable bride and then, after he has arranged a sham marriage with his tenant Wei-Wei, they arrive from China determined to organize a magnificent traditional wedding feast. They want to meet Wei-Wei's parents. A normal *North American* marriage is an arrangement between two individuals, but a *Chinese* marriage is a matter involving two large families, whose interests must be taken into account and whose "face" must be protected. Wai-Tung's father even hints to Simon that he knows about his son's homosexuality, but asks him not to reveal anything. After all, if it became known it would damage the reputation of the family!

2. Communication Style (High- *vs.* Low-Context)

In *Brick Lane* (dir. Sarah Gavron, United Kingdom 2007, analyzed by JANA SCHILLING), Nazneen, a *Bangladeshi* immigrant to Britain, meets her *Westernized* neighbor Razia. Razia smokes, has short hair, and talks a lot. She is better integrated into British society. The way that Razia opens herself up to Nazneen is more typical of a low-context Western culture than of a high-context Asian one, where first contacts would be more formal and you would not volunteer so much information about yourself to a near-stranger.

3. Time Management (Mono- *vs.* Polychronic)

In *Zorba the Greek* (dir. Michael Cacoyannis, USA / Greece 1964, analyzed by SIMONE PRAULICH), Zorba has agreed to build his British employer Basil a cable transportation system for his mine. But when Basil asks him how long he will need, Zorba becomes confused. The monochronic *Briton* needs to have deadlines, the polychronic *Greek* doesn't see the need for them. Zorba is sent into town with a list of things to do. Once in town, instead of sticking to the schedule and ticking off the items one by one in "efficient" monochronic fashion, Zorba follows his fancy and actually ends up spending Basil's money on girls and fun. He writes a letter to Basil, asking him why they should push things...

4. Time Orientation (Long- *vs.* Short-term)

In *Flags of Our Fathers* (dir. Clint Eastwood, USA 2006,

analyzed by ILIA BARANCIC), we see the *Americans* preparing for the assault on Iwo Jima, and the *Japanese* preparing for its defence. General Smith complains that he has only been given three days to "soften up" the Japanese with shelling, not the ten days that he asked for. At High Command they are impatient for results—although a too precipitate attack on the island will put many American lives at risk. The Japanese, in contrast, are shown carefully preparing the defences of the island many months in advance.

5. Interactive Style ("Masculine" or "Feminine")

In *What's Cooking?* (dir. Gurinder Chadha, United Kingdom / USA 2000, analyzed by MELIZE DA SILVA COLUCCI), set in Los Angeles, *Vietnamese-American* Jimmy is dating the *Mexican-American* Gina Avila. At the Avilas', Thanksgiving dinner is being prepared. Jimmy wanders into the kitchen, and the women joke about there being "a man in the kitchen". He goes back into the living room, where the men are all watching TV. Later Jimmy asks Gina's brother Tony whether the men shouldn't help the women a bit, but Tony rejects the idea. The gender roles in the Avila family are very distinct, with women doing the home-making, whereas among Vietnamese the gender roles tend to be less different.

> A society is called *masculine* when emotional gender roles are clearly distinct: men are supposed to be assertive, tough, and focused on material success, whereas women are supposed to be more modest, tender, and concerned with the quality of life.
> A society is called *feminine* when emotional gender roles overlap: both men and women are supposed to be modest, tender, and concerned with the quality of life (Hofstede / Hofstede 1991, 120, emphases in the original).

6. Power Distance (Power and Inequality)

In *Spanglish* (dir. James L. Brooks, USA 2004, analyzed by
DORTHE DALGAARD JENSEN and EWA ZATOŃSKA), the *Mexican-
American* Flor has come for an interview for a job as a house-
keeper. While her new employer, the *"Anglo"* Mrs. Clasky,
welcomes her with a hug, treats her virtually as an equal and
asks her to call her by her first name, Flor carefully keeps her
distance, addresses her respectfully as "Mrs. Clasky" and
returns her welcoming gesture with a handshake.

7. Proxemics (Space and Distance)

In *My Big Fat Greek Wedding* (dir. Joel Zwick, USA / Canada
2002, analyzed by CLAUDIA SCHUMACHER and EVA BERGOLD)
the *Greek-American* girl Toula falls in love with *"Anglo"* Ian.
When the young couple visit Ian's very middle-class parents,
notice how far apart they sit! But when Ian's parents are invited
to Toula's house for what is supposed to be just a quiet get-
together, they find the whole extended Greek family, cousins,
uncles, aunts, *etc.*, roasting a lamb in the front yard, and Toula's
father embarrasses them by invading their personal space and
hugging them enthusiastically.

8. Human Nature (Trust)

In *Outsourced* (dir. John Jeffcoat, India / USA 2006, analyzed
by KATRIN BONKAT), the *American* Todd almost misses his train
at the main railway station in Mumbai (Bombay). A friendly
Indian tells him to jump onto the moving train, which, with
some trepidation, he does—and the other passengers catch him
and pull him to safety. Todd is not used to being helped in a
situation like this; in the Western world people do not normally
trust strangers in this way.

9. Relationship to the Environment

In the thriller *Smilla's Sense of Snow* (dir. Bille August, Germany / Denmark / Sweden 1997, analyzed by ANKE DETTMAR), the whole plot turns on the remarkable ability of Smilla, a *Danish* girl brought up in Greenland, to understand ice and snow conditions just as the *Inuit* ("Eskimos") can. She has a quite un-European awareness of her natural environment, and can "read" marks in the snow that the Danish police cannot even see, let alone interpret.

10. Self-Identification (Doing *vs.* Being)

In *Urga* (dir. Nikita Mikhalkov, France / Soviet Union, 1991, analyzed by LEA DROLSHAGEN and BIRTE SECHTIG), the *Mongolian* Gombo goes to a club with his *Russian* friend Sergei. Sergei complains bitterly about how unsuccessful his life (as a trucker) is, how little he earns, how his wife will be ashamed of him because of this, and so on. He defines himself in terms of his job, "what he does", and how much money he has. Gombo offers to give him some money—for him, this is not the key to happiness in life, but he realizes how unhappy his friend is.

11. Motivation (Expressive *vs.* Instrumental)

In *Day for Night* (dir. François Truffaut, France 1973, analyzed by NINA WIESSNER), the spoilt, immature young actor Alphonse throws a fit and threatens to sabotage the film production that he is involved in. His colleagues try without success to mollify him. His British co-star Julie wins him round by sleeping with him. She has no feelings for him, and is risking her own (happy) marriage, but, in the face of so much *French* emotionality, with characteristic *British* middle-class *sang-froid* and common sense she makes a decision of the head, not the heart, to do what needs to be done to save the film project.

12. Uncertainty Avoidance

In *Night on Earth* (dir. Jim Jarmusch, USA 1991, analyzed by INGA BARTELT), the *German* Helmut is enjoying his first day as a taxi-driver in *New York*. Unfortunately, he doesn't know how to drive an automatic car. When his passenger YoYo, worried about whether they are ever going to reach Brooklyn, offers to do the driving for him, Helmut is unwilling to go against the rules and regulations. YoYo explains to him that it's OK—take a risk, this is New York!—and introduces him to the pragmatic way that they do things in the Big Apple.

13. Task- *vs.* Person-Orientation

In *Midnight in the Garden of Good and Evil* (dir. Clint Eastwood, USA 1997, analyzed by ANNE SCHULZ and ROLAND KEMMER), set in Savannah, Georgia, the brash young *New York* journalist John tries to interview the exotic Lady Chablis. The Lady is in mourning, but John is determined to get his interview and knocks insistently on her door. Only when she locks it ostentatiously loudly does he finally show some respect for her privacy. In the course of the film, John learns (from the Lady, among other characters) to understand the more tactful, indirect, mannered and person-oriented culture of *the South*.

14. Achieved *vs.* Ascribed Status

In *The Beauty of Sin* (dir. Živko Nikolić, Yugoslavia 1986, analyzed by FRANCIS JARMAN), the young couple Luka and Jaglika leave their conservative, backward village to seek their fortune in a modern, decadent holiday resort on the coast. The man who lures them into making this move, and then exploits them shamelessly, selling their labor and trying to pimp Luka to a wealthy homosexual, is their "friend" George. He was the best man at their wedding, and is consequently ascribed a unique status in their lives, whereas in reality he is an opportunistic crook who has done nothing to deserve their trust. The contrast in cultural attitudes here is between traditional *Montenegrin village culture* and sophisticated, urbanized *Yugoslav* (and "Western") culture.

15. Diffuse *vs.* Specific Identity

In *The Year of Living Dangerously* (dir. Peter Weir, Australia 1982, analyzed by INA SIEBALD), set in Indonesia, the *Australian* journalist Guy is asked for money by the sister of his assistant, Kumar; she tells Guy that her brother has financial problems. Guy is willing to help. He understands the local *Indonesian* way of doing things, how the boss always remains the boss, and boss and subordinates will help and support each other outside the work situation as well as within it. Ironically, Kumar is very unwilling to accept Guy's help: he is a Communist, with "modern" (*i.e.*, Western) rather than traditional ideas about social relationships.

16. Universalism *vs.* Particularism

In *Under the Tuscan Sun* (dir. Audrey Wells, USA / Italy 2003, analyzed by DOMINIKA LUKOSZEK and BERENIKE KUSCHEL), the *American* Frances, who is visiting Rome, meets a charming *Italian*, Marcello, who drives her down to Positano to look for a particular antique furniture shop. On the way, she learns how Italians see the role of rules and laws, for instance traffic lights: "green: *avanti, avanti*!, yellow: decoration, red: just a suggestion..." In other words, in particularist Italy it is not the abstract rules that matter, but the needs of the specific situation, to which people adjust their behavior as they see fit.

17. Formality

In *Lost in Translation* (dir. Sofia Coppola, USA 2003, analyzed by ANN ECKERT and IRIS KOHLER), set in Japan, the *American*

Bob takes part in the shooting of a commercial for whisky. He is nonplussed that the English translations of the *Japanese* explanations are always much shorter. This is because Japanese use more "honorifics" and formal expressions when addressing people, and therefore often require longer to say things than English speakers do.

18. Front- *vs.* Backstage Cultures

In *Black Rain* (dir. Ridley Scott, USA / Japan 1989, analyzed by ANDRÉ SCHWENTUCHOWSKI), the *American* policemen Nick and Charlie take part in a meeting with *Japanese* police officers at Osaka police headquarters. The Americans are used to talking loudly, freely, and a lot (and the more important you are, the more you will normally feel that you are expected to say), but the behavior of the Japanese is not so straightforward and "frontstage", what you see is *not* necessarily what you get, and it is difficult for the Americans to interpret the situation, work out what is going on and (for instance) tell who the "boss" is.

19. Affectivity (Emotion Management)

In *The White Masai* (dir. Hermine Huntgeburth, Germany 2005, analyzed by RAÉLA HAGEMANN), the *Swiss* girl Carola has fallen in love with an illiterate Kenyan *Samburu* warrior named Lemalian, married him and gone to live with him in his village. Carola and Lemalian are visiting Nairobi: Carola goes to the bank, and laughs happily while she is talking to the cashier. Her husband asks her whether she knows the man, and cannot understand why she was laughing with a stranger. The Samburu don't show their emotions openly, especially not to strangers. A Samburu woman is not even allowed to show that she is in pain during childbirth. When Carola has a baby, the nurse covers her mouth when she cries out.

20. Traditionalism *vs.* Secularism

Le thé au harem d'Archimède (dir. Mehdi Charef, France 1985, analyzed by JOHANNA HOEFER and FELICITAS QUASS) reveals the lives of immigrants in Paris, torn between their traditional *North African* culture on the one hand and modern *French* values and behavior on the other. Madjid's mother is shown praying in the prescribed manner, but with loud pop music playing in the background. She is trying to keep up the traditional ways, but her children have become more or less attuned to life to France, as shown by their noisy music and lack of respect for their mother's prayers.

IT IS RECOGNIZED that some of the cultural dimensions correlate or overlap with each other. Brief descriptions of the dimensions can be found on the website, under "Glossary". An additional (twenty-first) item, "Miscellaneous", provides a convenient heading under which unfamiliar ethnographic material can be explained. The catalog of dimensions is work in progress, and should be understood as a practical analytical tool rather than as a fixed taxonomy of cultural-descriptive categories.

The database, which can be searched by feature (such as "culture" or "cultural dimension") or by a full-text search, at the time of writing contains analyses of well over a hundred films, with many more in preparation.

The intention behind the project has right from the beginning been to provide a useful resource for teachers, lecturers or discussion leaders who need attractive material to illustrate intercultural communication situations. There are many individual works on the "intercultural film", but most of them fall into one of two categories: they are either intellectually and technically demanding investigations of the way in which films create meaning, or they are studies of the manipulative Western discourse of non-Western cultures (the first and probably still the best of these being Harold R. Isaacs' *Scratches on Our Minds*, 1958; a more recent study is Jaap van Ginneken's *Screening*

Difference: How Hollywood's Blockbuster Films Imagine Race, Ethnicity and Culture, 2007).

There are also writers like Ellen Summerfield who have followed a more practical approach (Summerfield 1993, Summerfield / Lee 2006, *etc.*), though these books tend to have a very strong American focus and an obsession with issues of prejudice and discrimination. They offer—along with teaching suggestions—Mostly ethnographic, historical and background information, rather than analysis of cultural behavior or discussion of the reasons for intercultural communication breakdown.

In order to reach a wide international audience the website is in English, and the movies chosen for analysis are Mostly those that are available on DVD with either an English-language option or English subtitles, though some exceptions have been made. The project could easily be widened to include TV films and series that meet these criteria.

The IcFilmDB project has been presented at universities and conferences in many countries, including Germany, Hungary and the United States. Several other universities have shown interest in joining the project, and a collaboration has already begun with Lindsey Wilson College in Kentucky. The IcFilmDB has been honored by being included on *Intute*, an online service providing "access to the very best Web resources for education and research, selected and evaluated by a network of subject specialists". *Intute* is sponsored by a consortium of seven major British universities (Birmingham, Bristol, Heriot-Watt, Manchester, Manchester MU, Nottingham and Oxford) and is funded by the British Joint Information Systems Committee (JISC).

References

Barnes, Julian. "Subcontinental Soap." In: *The Observer*, May 4th, 1986, 26.

Beneke, Jürgen. *Orientation Matrix: The 14 Dimensions of Culure*. Working Paper, The University of Hildesheim

Research Center for Intercultural Communication, February 2001. Website, <http://www.uni-hildesheim.de/~beneke/SS04/Vorlesung/Cultural Dimensions.pdf>

Ginneken, Jaap van. *Screening Difference: How Hollywood's Blockbuster Films Imagine Race, Ethnicity and Culture.* Lanham, MD: Rowman & Littlefield, 2007.

Hildesheim Intercultural Film Database, The. Website, <http://www.uni-hildesheim.de/interculturalfilm/index.php>

Hofstede, Geert / Hofstede, Gert Jan. *Cultures and Organizations: Software of the Mind* (1991). Second edition. New York: McGraw-Hill, 2005.

Isaacs, Harold R. *Scratches on Our Minds: American Images of China & India.* New York: John Day, 1958.

Jarman, Francis. "Der Interkulturelle Film—eine neue Datenbank an der Universität Hildesheim." In: *Uni Hildesheim: Das Magazin,* 11, December 2006, 17 f.

------------. The Hildesheim Intercultural Film Database. In: *Methodische Vielfalt in der Erforschung interkultureller Kommunikation an deutschen Hochschulen.* Proceedings of a conference held at the Institute of Intercultural Communication, University of Hildesheim, October 15th-17th, 2009. Ed. Elke Bosse / Beatrix Kress / Stephan Schlickau. Frankfurt/M.: Lang, 2011, 257.

Rushdie, Salman. "The Raj Revival." In: *The Observer,* April 1st, 1984, 19.

Summerfield, Ellen. *Crossing Cultures through Film.* Yarmouth, MN: Intercultural Press, 1993.

------------ / Lee, Sandra. *Seeing the Big Picture: A Cinematic Aproach to Understanding Cultures in America.* Ann Arbor, MI: University of Michigan Press, 2006.

Appendix: Western Actors, Asian Roles

Rex Harrison as the King of Siam, **Lee J. Cobb** (in grotesque make-up) as the Prime Minister, and **Linda Darnell** as the Siamese slave-girl Tuptim in *Anna and the King of Siam* (1946)

Jean Simmons as an Indian nymphomaniac in *Black Narcissus* (1947)

Orson Welles as the famous Mongol general Bayan in *The Black Rose* (1950)

Tyrone Power as a very light-skinned Eurasian ("Anglo-Indian" is the polite term in India) in *King of the Khyber Rifles* (1953)

Richard Burton as an Indian doctor in *The Rains of Ranchipur* (1955)

Jennifer Jones with skilful make-up but, with her un-Oriental manner and appearance, miscast as a Eurasian doctor in *Love is a Many-Splendored Thing* (1955)

Lee J. Cobb (again) as a Chinese warlord in *The Left Hand of God* (1955)

Ava Gardner somewhat more convincing as the Eurasian girl in *Bhowani Junction* (1956), with **Francis Matthews** as her Indian boyfriend Ranjit

Marlon Brando, in heavy make-up, twitching and grimacing as an Okinawan interpreter in *The Teahouse of the August Moon* (1956)

Yul Brynner as the King of Siam in *The King and I* (1956)

Giorgia Moll as the Vietnamese girl in *The Quiet American* (1958)

Western actors playing all (?) of the Japanese roles in *The Camp on Blood Island* (1958)

Herbert Lom as the villainous Muslim journalist in *Northwest Frontier* (1959)

Curd Jurgens as a Eurasian general and **Robert Donat** as a Chinese mandarin in *The Inn of the Sixth Happiness* (1959)

Alec Guinness as a Japanese businessman in *A Majority of One*

(1961)

Flora Robson and **Robert Helpmann** as the Chinese villains in the historical epic *55 Days at Peking* (1963)

Horst Buchholz as the Indian fanatic who assassinated Gandhi, in *Nine Hours to Rama* (1963)

Laurence Harvey as the half-Chinese Ivan in *A Girl Named Tamiko* (1963)

Capucine as the Eurasian "love-interest" in *The Seventh Dawn* (1964)

Anthony Quinn as Kublai Khan in *Marco the Magnificent* (1964)

Robert Morley as the Emperor of China and **James Mason** as a Chinese prince in *Genghis Khan* (1965)

Yul Brynner (again) as an Indian bandit chief in *The Long Duel* (1967)

Ben Kingsley in the title role of *Gandhi* (1982)

Amy Irving as Princess Anjuli in *The Far Pavilions* (1983)

Alec Guinness (again) as Professor Godbole in *A Passage to India* (1984)

A particularly weird case is that of the film *My Geisha* (1962), in which a director, searching in Japan for a suitable girl to play Madame Butterfly in his forthcoming movie of the opera, picks his own wife (played by **Shirley Maclaine**), who has disguised herself as a *geisha* so convincingly (yes, Shirley Maclaine, *really*) that she wins the role.

CASTING SHOWS AND CULTURE

HOW NATIONAL CULTURE DEFINES WHO WINS AND WHO LOSES ON *POP IDOL*

by ANNE-KRISTIN LANGNER

"I think that by ignoring the show you're ignoring the audience who put you there."

—Simon Cowell,
British television producer

POP IDOL IS one of the world's most famous casting formats. First launched in Great Britain in 2001, it has spread all over the globe and became one of the most popular TV shows worldwide. Although the standardized format has its cross-national rules and regulations, the national spin-offs often have distinctive national characteristics. To be more explicit—national cultural ideals and valuess define who will win or lose on *Pop Idol*.

The research done so far on international TV formats like *Pop Idol* has often been focused more on economic factors than on the cultural background of the corresponding spin-off. Using statistical data to explain the success story of *Pop Idol*, which has been sold to more than fifty countries, is a common approach. What is usually missing in studies of *Pop Idol* is the meaning behind those numbers. My paper focuses on the meaning and excludes the figures, and the analysis of meaning is based on culture. The data that I use are therefore of a qualitative, narrative nature. The interviewees are asked to describe their way of watching the show, what they feel, how they would explain certain situations on stage, and so on. This way of collecting data enables me to understand not only the functional ideas of the interviewees but also their aesthetic views. The researcher, in advance, has to acquire a comprehensive knowledge of the format; and so a high level of information is needed. The initial approach is hermeneutic, and includes watching episodes and analyzing the script and the staging completely, so that the researcher will be able to understand the interviewees' statements. Since there is no communication without context, it is not sufficient for an all-inclusive analysis to collect only statistical data. This merely leads to a general impression of the show that will not be sufficient for forming a basis for conclusions. I would argue that the aesthetic interpretations that I am going to suggest here have not in the past been given proper attention. Understanding the meaning that people ascribe to the show will help us to understand the significance of the show in general. Working solely on the economic level will only provide information on the show's structural framework.

The empirical basis for this paper is two interviews with German viewers and fans of the German spin-off of *Pop Idol*, each lasting a good three hours.

The format *Pop Idol* is a so-called "real-people-format". This kind of format offers new possibilities with regard to the international trade in and the adaptation of formats. This growing diversification in the production of TV entertainment is called *factual entertainment*, a term deriving from an Anglo-American source. In contrast to Reality TV in *Big Brother*-style, where people essentially carry on with their every-day lives, but in a container, factual entertainment formats like *Pop Idol* go much further. The format suggests that people will have the opportunity to really change their lives, and that they might enjoy a successful career and a new life afterwards. That helps to keep people interested in the show even after the actual broadcasting time. Moreover, the product environment is fully included in the staging (Göttlich 2004, 125 f.). Factual entertainment productions, in contrast to Reality TV, enable the audience to intervene and to have a personal impact on the show, which is very important for a cultural approach, as we will see later.

A format that is categorized as factual entertainment can be seen as consisting of a mixture of entertainment, information and human fate, presented and staged on television (Döveling *et al.* 2007, 110). And once we are concerned with human fate, it becomes impossible to ignore culture and society, with all the ideas and values that these entail, in analyzing *Pop Idol*.

As the term real-people-format implies, we are now involved with *people*. With regard to *Pop Idol*, it means that we have a jury, an anchorman, the candidates and the audience at home and in the studio. What sounds so trivial is actually most important here. A get-together of people is always characterized by the culture(s) that they belong to, meaning that there are certain ways of communicating, certain ideas about behavior or, in general, values and ideas, that one is geared to. Defining culture is notoriously difficult. As early as the Fifties, there were already more than two hundred definitions of culture in circulation and the range of definitions is wide, stretching from the aesthetic-textual to anthropological definitions in terms of the common behavior patterns of people (Grossberg 1999, 21). Since this paper is about national cultures and the way that people belonging to them behave towards *Pop Idol* candidates, the definition given in Hofstede / Hofstede (2005) would be an appropriate one to quote in this context:

> Culture is always a collective phenomenon, because it is at least partly shared with people who live or lived within the same social environment, which is where it was learned. Culture consists of the unwritten rules of the social game. It is *the collective programming of the*

mind that distinguishes the members of one group or category of people from others.

Culture is learned, not innate. It derives from one's social environment rather than from one's genes. Culture should be distinguished from human nature on one side and from an individual's personality on the other [...] (4, emphasis in the original).

The distinction between human culture, human nature and individual personality is important. *Human nature* is that which all human beings have in common, *i.e.*, what is inherited with one's genes, for example being able to feel fear or love or having the facility to observe the environment. *Individual personality*, in contrast, refers to people's behavioral uniqueness. Everybody has special traits that are not necessarily shared with others and which derive from the interplay of the *culture* (or cultures) that they live in and their own personal experiences (Hofstede / Hofstede, 4 f.). Although this paper will only refer to national cultures, it is important to mention that people can belong to more than one culture, of which there are many types, having, for instance, a job culture, deriving from their working environment, in addition to their national culture. Such a listing of different cultures is given by (among others) Laine-Sveiby (1987, 11 f.):

> *Varje grupp med självaktning kan hänvisa till sin speciella form av kultur. Vi pratar om yrkeskulturer, lokalkulturer, fabrikskulturer, företagskulturer och [...] om nationella kulturer.*
>
> ("Every group with self-respect can point to their special form of culture. We talk about job cultures, local cultures, industrial cultures, organizational cultures and [...] national cultures" [my translation]).

Her listing is by no means exhaustive—some scholars would also include gender cultures, generational cultures and subcultures, for example.

To analyze and interpret the cultural behavior of fans towards their *Pop Idol* stars, it is necessary to categorize the traits of a national culture. This enables us to say *how* and *why* cultures are different and behave differently and not merely *that* they are different (Gudykunst / Young 1984, 42). In his *Cultures and Organizations*, Hofstede defined five determinant dimensions in national cultures. Between 1967 and 1973 he interviewed IBM employees in 66 countries to find out more about their cultural conditioning. The Hofstede dimensions are: Power Distance, Individualism versus Collectivism, Masculinity versus Femininity, Avoidance of Uncertainty, and Long- versus Short-term Orientation. In the empirical data that I collected in two qualitative interviews on the German spin-off of *Pop Idol*, Individualism versus Collectivism was the most outstanding dimension. Therefore the analysis is based on this dimension, which Hofstede defines as follows:

> *Individualism* pertains to *societies in which the ties between individuals are loose: everyone is expected to look after himself or herself and his or her immediate family. Collectivism* as its opposite pertains to *societies in which people from birth onward are integrated into strong, cohesive in-groups, which throughout people's lifetimes continue to protect them in exchange for unquestioning loyalty* (Hofstede / Hofstede, 76, emphases in the original).

Hofstede applied his results on cultural dimensions to a number of areas of human life, including occupation, the family, school, the workplace and the state. But what is missing in all studies on cultural standards and characteristics is a connection between cultural behavior and the use of the media, for instance, the behavior of viewers of *Pop Idol*. The discussion up to now has tended to emphasize economic factors This is not to say that they are never significant. For example: why does America often enable its superstar to live the American dream, "to rise from rags to riches", while not one of the German winners could successfully initiate some kind of longer-lasting career? It so happens that the winner of *American Idol* normally enjoys outstanding marketing. Successful candidates from *Deutschland sucht den Superstar*, on the other hand, have difficulties selling their music due to the fact that German radio stations refuse to play their songs. It's as simple as that.

Nevertheless, the assumption made in this paper is that the behavior of *Pop Idol* fans towards their favored candidate, during the program's seasonal run and immediately afterwards, is, to a great extent, connected with Hofstede's Individualism versus Collectivism dimension.

Bearing in mind the influence of culture on the audience's behavior and reactions, we should take a short look at the development of the "real-people-format". From the Eighties onward, the development of television formats and genres became more and more differentiated and offered new possibilities (Göttlich 2004, 124 f.), for instance, for combining information and entertainment, facts and fiction. Furthermore, the audience at home was offered new possibilities to participate, actively or by proxy. In the case of *Pop Idol*, active participation means the chance to join in through telephone voting. Every candidate who participates gets his or her own phone extension and SMS code, and members of the audience are invited by the jury members or the anchorman to make a call or send a text message to their favorites. The number of phone calls and SMS messages is crucial— the candidate with the most calls and messages will be the next superstar. Participation by proxy, on the other hand, is realized through the candidate performing on stage. Since everybody has the chance to take part in a *Pop Idol* casting, the candidate on stage represents the people sitting in front of the television ("this could have been me"), who can live out their own dream by proxy through their favorite.

Der musikalische Erfolg der Kandidaten, den sie nach *Deutschland sucht den Superstar* anstreben, stand hierbei nicht im Mittelpunkt—es ging in der Sendung um den Traum vom "Star-Werden". Diesen Traum lebten die Kandidaten mit den Zuschauern. Aufmerksamkeit, Anschlusskommunikation und vor allem das Televoting der Zuschauer zeugen vermeintlich davon, sie sind die wahren Stars (Döveling *et al.* 2007, 114).

("It was not the success in music that the candidates strive for after they have finished *Deutschland sucht den Superstar* that took center stage, but the dream of becoming a star. The candidates lived this dream with the audience. Attention, follow-up communication and above all the audience's televoting testify to that. The members of the audience are the real stars" [my translation].)

Audience members being called the real stars leads us back to the idea of individualism. Germany has been described as one of the more individualistic cultures (Hofstede / Hofstede, 78), and the philosophy of individualism is seen as very positive by many Germans. If everybody strives for satisfaction of their personal needs, it will automatically have a positive impact on society, too. This is a win-win situation (Trompenaars / Hampden-Turner 2005, 56), and it is the case with *Pop Idol*, too. From their individualistic point of view, Germans choose the candidate they like best. He or she is then the one who lives out for them the dream of becoming a star. The candidate, on the other hand, benefits from the phone calls and SMS messages enabling him or her to complete show after show successfully. Special arrangements are made for televoting. In Germany, every call or SMS costs fifty Eurocents. The price for a phone call or SMS to support a candidate differs from country to country. In the United States the voting is sometimes even free of charge.

Both interviewees agreed that you are not only supporting

but actually *buying* "your" star, which puts you in the position of having certain expectations. With perfect staging, the candidates are literally put under the spotlight. From the "top fifteen" onward, the shows are organized according to a specific motto: ballad, rock, "German songs", and so on. Both interviewees said that the candidates then had no chance to show their personal style and to sing in the manner that fitted them best. The staging is so elaborate and striking that a candidate's personality may be completely submerged. In addition, the members of the jury help to set a particular tone through their direct and critical comments. The audience's disappointment after the series has ended is often obvious. One of the interviewees claimed that her favorite, whose style and image during the show was this of a ballad singer, started performing some kind of "house" music after the show had ended. The interviewee felt mocked, that she had been "taken for a ride", and lost her faith in the candidate— he no longer lived up to the distinctive and individualistic ideas that she had had about him.

Both these points—having such expectations of a candidate, but also looking for a candidate who has a strong personality— are homologous with German individualism. The members of the audience want the candidates to show their character, and show that they are willing to be polarizing figures, since everybody has his or her own individualistic character that should not be hidden. Fighting for your personal ideals is strongly encouraged: "In order to demonstrate who they are, Germans are known to argumentatively fight for their position and to show self-assertion" (Schroll-Machl 2003, 173).

That does not, of course, necessarily lead to the formation of a strong fan group, and it can even result in the formation of a group of anti-fans or hecklers who, for instance, boo when the candidate comes onto the stage or clap when the judgment by the jury members is particularly abusive.

The members of the jury, who are honest and rigorous in their assessments, are individualistic, too. Being nice to one candidate and hard on another puts these on different levels that reflect the jury members' personal views and opinions. This is different, however, in Sweden. Sweden is an individualistic society, too, but because of their history and social system the Swedes are at the same time very egalitarian (Robinowitz / Carr 2001, 57). Everybody gets the same chance. Judgment is very objective and concentrates on the performance. But it is also less strict, so as not to treat people differently and unequally.

In Germany, once you have found your personal favorite, it is accepted, in fact even expected, that you will become a fan of theirs and express dislike of the other candidates. Fans tend to be dismissed as being simply passive consumers of products, but in Cultural Studies they are often seen more positively, as active participants in a process, acquiring products and producing cultural meaning (Göttlich / Krischke-Ramaswamy 2003, 167 f.). To appreciate the (cultural) meaning that fans ascribe to *Pop Idol*, it is necessary to approach the phenomenon from an aesthetic rather than an economic perspective. Understanding the aesthetic propositions, the scripts and the staging of *Pop Idol* enables the researcher to understand and evaluate the answers produced in the qualitative interviews and to discover cultural ideals. It is not enough just to look at the development of audience ratings and marketing strategies. The fans are not there simply to help the TV stations to earn money—they create *meaning*. And their cultural background is an important factor in that process: it is what determines who wins and who loses on *Pop Idol*.

References

Döveling, Katrin / Kurotschka, Mara / Nieland, Jörg-Uwe. "*Deutschland sucht den Superstar*. Hintergründe einer Erfolgsgeschichte." In: *Im Namen des Fernsehvolkes: Neue Formate für Orientierung und Bewertung.* Ed. Katrin Döveling / Lothar Mikos / Jörg-Uwe Nieland. Konstanz: UVK, 2007, 103-16.

Göttlich, Udo. "Produzierte Wirklichkeiten: Zur Entwicklung der Fernsehproduktion am Beispiel von Factual Entertainment

Angeboten." In: *Diversifikation in der Unterhaltungsproduktion.* Ed. Mike Friedrichsen / Udo Göttlich. Cologne: Herbert von Halem, 2004, 124-41.

------------ / Krischke-Ramaswamy, Mohini. "Fan". In: *Handbuch Populäre Kultur: Begriffe, Theorien und Diskussionen.* Ed. Hans-Otto Hügel. Stuttgart: J. B. Metzler, 2003, 167-72.

Grossberg, Lawrence. "Der Cross Road Blues der Cultural Studies." In: *Kultur-Medien-Macht: Cultural Studies und Medienanalyse.* Ed. Andreas Hepp / Rainer Winter. Second edition. Opladen: Westdeutscher Verlag, 1999, 15-31.

Gudykunst, William B. / Kim, Young Yun. *Communicating with Strangers: An Approach to Intercultural Communication* (1984). Second edition. New York: McGraw-Hill, 1992.

Hofstede, Geert / Hofstede, Gert Jan. *Cultures and Organizations: Software of the Mind* (1991). Second edition. New York: McGraw-Hill, 2005.

Laine-Sveiby, Kati. *Svenskhet som strategi.* Stockholm: Timbro, 1987.

Robinowitz, Christina Johansson / Carr, Lisa Werner. *Modern-Day Vikings: A Practical Guide to Interacting with the Swedes.* Yarmouth, MN: Intercultural Press, 2001.

Schroll-Machl, Sylvia. *Doing Business with Germans: Their Perception, Our Perception.* Göttingen: Vandenhoeck & Ruprecht, 2003.

Trompenaars, Fons / Hampden-Turner, Charles. *Riding the Waves of Culture: Understanding Cultural Diversity in Business.* Expanded edition of Trompenaars' 1993 publication. London: Nicholas Brealey, 2005.

GROWING "OTHER"WISE

by MANJU RAMANAN

THIS PAPER AIMS to discuss the issue of censorship—state-enforced, publisher-enforced and self-imposed—on the production of some news, features and articles published in the United Arab Emirates (UAE) and India. Often accused of "churnalism"—which may be described as a form of journalism in which press releases, wire stories, and other forms of pre-packaged material are used to create articles in newspapers and other news media in order to meet increasing pressures of time and cost without undertaking further research or checking (see Monck 2008)—the media industry in the UAE is known to operate under the rigid control of media laws or as per the advertiser's demands, and in some cases punitive action is taken against the editor or the publishing house for an objectionable article. However, there are several examples in Indian journalism or Indo-British collaborative journalism that reflects a kind of control in writing. We shall explore these varied kinds of "ordered writings", which are not exclusive to the UAE.

As a practicing journalist in the UAE, I see writers with two sides to them: their personalities that come forth through their writings and what they actually are and state when unconfronted by the pressure to print. Like many others, I see myself becoming an "other". Or, like my colleagues, I start inventing and crafting that "other". But is this "other" not constructed in regions that claim that the media are unfettered and unchained? As a journalist in India, working for a "well-known daily" as well as for a "popular women's magazine", I have often crafted this "other". By "other" I mean the process of construing and constructing a print personality of the writer that doesn't necessarily reflect the writer's own ideology. This "other" is created because of various factors—censorship, the ideology of the market, the philosophy of the media organization. My impressions of this creation of "other" derive heavily from my own career as a journalist in India and the UAE.

With the largest number of young people in the world, India has many newspapers, magazines and tabloids that aim to attract the young, a policy that is also mentored to the editorial teams by the marketing departments of some of the newspapers. This fetish about writing around themes centered on "the young" is a policy drilled into writers by the marketing, brand management and circulation teams. Contributing to an article, for a renowned women's magazine, about women travelling alone, I interviewed a woman of about forty; it was then politely suggested that I call her back and ask her if we could describe her as being eight years younger! The ideology of the magazine was to "reflect", I was told, and we were to try to attract the young. The readers would apparently prefer to discover a 32-year-old being quoted in the article rather than a forty-year-old. This would also fulfill the magazine's brand management team directives and its requirements—which influence editorial policy. When I made the call, dreading a showdown at the other end, the subject gladly agreed to my request, and the job was carried out swiftly. Call it "ageist"—from "ageism", a term meaning "discrimination against people based on age" that was coined by the US gerontologist Robert N. Butler in 1969—or clipping facts to suit the profile of the magazine, it prompted the creation of the "other", this time by consent of the subject interviewed.

Often in editorial meetings for the magazine we were asked to mentally map the woman we were writing for. She was obviously not the girl next door, but a cool, sassy, sexy, confident woman, who dressed immaculately, ate at the best places in town, shopped well, and knew exactly how to take care of herself and her family. We spent hours building this woman up by words and descriptions—often drawing upon instances from real life, listing various attributes that would be in sync with the magazine's ideology—and came up with a list of her various lifestyle attributes, including the places where she shopped, the credit cards she carried, the salary she earned, the countries she traveled to, the children she had or had adopted, her personal space, the man in her life (we were told that the term "husband" had become outdated), the unique way she balanced her family and work and managed to look groomed and attractive, and so on. As we collated these various opinions, we realized that such a woman didn't exist. We had created a complete "other"—who represented *aspiration*. She was the ideal that couldn't be real. She couldn't be someone you knew—she was someone who was unattainable. While women would dream of being like her, men would dream of a woman like her or want the woman in their life to be like her. Air-brushed photographs played a very important role in creating this "other", and we learned why many glossies around the world attach huge importance to photographs, which help in reinforcing the "other", increasing the appeal to a mass readership that is often ignorant or unaware of such a strategy: a strategy in which "subliminal seduction" (see Key 1974 and Molis) is always involved.

In the state of Gujarat in Western India, where drinking alcohol is prohibited under the law but available in abundance, we often, in the press room, screened photographs of a Page 3 booze party and color-corrected the liquor in it to appear like a glass of water or a "mocktail". This practice is also carried out in Dubai, which has stringent rules about printing pictures of alcohol, since the state's religion forbids it. The UAE has several night clubs and an active night life with free-flowing alcohol, but none of the happenings surrounding them ever make it to being newspaper news—except maybe drunken driving, a drunken brawl or a swoop on an illegal booze supply booth. Similarly, the life of a bar girl or the happenings at a bar would never be newsworthy, but reports on legal action against the sexual exploitation of bar girls surely would, as would raids on the numerous brothels spread across the country.

Journalism in the UAE is looked down upon by a whole lot of press people, as well as by the general public. In popular parlance, it is even called a journalist's graveyard because there is strict control of what can be printed. But it is also important to remember that the institution of a free press is largely a feature of democratic countries, and the UAE is a sheikhdom, so the comparison falls rather flat. Also, the model that the UAE press subscribes to is that of a family and it is patriarchally understood and accepted that you don't speak out against your family to outsiders—in this case, the outside world.

The UAE consists of seven emirates, Dubai, Abu Dhabi (the capital), Sharjah, Ajman, Umm ul Quwain, Ras Al Khaimah and Fujairah, and became a federation in the Seventies, before which it was part of what the British called the Trucial States (Joyce 1999). Each emirate is governed by a ruler, with the ruling family getting the prime portfolios in the governance process. The rulers form the Supreme Council of the UAE. Right from the earliest days of the federation until today, the ruler of Abu Dhabi has been the President of the UAE and the ruler of Dubai the Vice-President. The rest of the emirates are represented on the Federal National Council.

The history of the media in the UAE is a fairly short one. In fact, *Gulf News* in a tabloid form (it later became a daily broadsheet) was only launched on September 30th, 1978 (*The History of Gulf News*, website), the *Khaleej Times*, the first English newspaper to be launched in the UAE, in the same year (Website); both started from Dubai. The latest newspaper to join them is *The National* from Abu Dhabi Media, launched in April 2008 (Website). As well as the newspapers, the UAE has several tabloids, magazines and newsletters covering various subjects ranging from lifestyle to banking and business. A large part of the media business is concentrated in Dubai and in Dubai Media City, which was set up by HH Sheikh Mohammed bin

Rashid Al Maktoum, Ruler of Dubai.

With regard to censorship, according to Wikipedia ("Communications in the United Arab Emirates"), on November 16th, 2007, the Dubai government

> ordered Tecom to shut down the popular independent Pakistani news channels *Geo News* and *ARY One World* on the demand of Pakistan's military regime led by General Pervez Musharraf. This was implemented by du Samacom disabling their SDI & ASI streams. Later policy makers in Dubai permitted these channels to air their entertainment programs, but news, current affairs and political analysis were forbidden. Although subsequently the conditions were removed, marked differences have since been observed in their coverage. This incident has had a serious impact on all organizations in the media city with *Geo TV* and *ARY OneWorld* considering relocation.

On April 13th, 2008, Du (EITC)—which is the second telecommunications operator in the UAE—announced that all of its traffic would be routed via the UAE's censorship proxy, which blocks access to any content deemed "inappropriate". While Dubai Internet City sells itself as a business-friendly environment with excellent connectivity, the reality is that it is heavily censored.

There is no dearth of information in the UAE press about road accidents, suicides, deaths, smuggled animals, raids on hotels serving unhygienic food, loose behavior, prostitution, sodomy, thievery, bank defaulters, corrupt officials, and so on. In fact, some of these horrors and outrages are covered in amazing detail—the most recent ones being the death of the Lebanese singer Suzanne Tamim, who was murdered in her plush Jumeirah apartment in 2008, and the killing of Hamas leader Mahmoud Al Mabhouh in Dubai on January 19th at the Al Bustan Rotana Hotel. (This latter operation has been widely attributed to Israel's Mossad intelligence service. Mabhouh had played a pivotal role in the Palestinian uprising in the Eighties.)

These two instances have been selected as examples because the media chose to highlight the alertness of the authorities in tracking down the killers in no time. The media adopt a congratulatory stance, conveying the message that the country will not tolerate miscreants and will come down heavily on nefarious activities. This also includes playing moral censor to stereotypical "western behavior", such as that of a British couple who were found having sex on a beach in Jumeirah during working hours, inviting the wrath of the authorities as well as that of those expatriates who look down on non-conservative dress and manners.

Another remarkable aspect of journalism in the UAE is the extreme care taken to spell out the names of the rulers and the ruling families with certain protocols that include "His Highness" for the ruler, a title extended to the ruler's sons and grandsons too, while "His Excellency" is a term used to address the heads of departments, *etc*. Both titles are applicable to the women in the royal families too. This includes deceased rulers. While writing a book called *Golden Tribute* on the late HH Sheikh Saqr bin Mohammed Al Qasimi, former ruler of Ras Al Khaimah (he was still alive when the book was published), I learnt all about the protocol, which is followed very strictly.

The book begins with the photograph of the ruler and an article about him, followed by articles about and photographs of the crown prince and deputy ruler. Then come his brothers, step-brothers, other family members, and the children by age, designation and position or sometimes according to the ruler's likes and dislikes. Relatives who had fallen out with the ruler were left out of the selection process. The omission extended to photographs of them as well as photographs of their close friends.

It is normal that, during the course of an interview, people express opinions freely yet later, when it comes to material being printed, insist on reviewing every word. A common practice in the UAE is for a copy of the article to be requested for review by a client, an advertiser or an interviewee, and it is then printed only after approval has been given—a process that sometimes goes back and forth several times. Since this is the norm followed, the process of censorship starts with the writer—who has already excluded words, phrases and information that might be found objectionable. Then, the reviewer edits it further and what comes back for printing is a copy that is usually full of superlatives.

It is not as if the leadership is completely intolerant of criticism. Readers' letters to newspapers are often full of complaints about the bad service provided by companies, non-remittance of funds, sewage problems, flaws they have encountered, *etc.*— and these complaints are followed up, too. But if you compare this with what happens in other parts of the world, where people are ready to take on the system, you'll not find it here. The UAE press cannot be compared to media elsewhere. But it is an evolving process, and should be watched carefully before hasty conclusions are drawn. It would be right to say that it makes a point of depicting the positive side of things more vigorously since it cannot compromise on its image. An image that runs its economy. An image that keeps the investments pouring in. HH Sheikh Mohammed bin Rashid Al Maktoum, the ruler of Dubai, has a Facebook profile and people of the emirate write to him. Started in 2009, it also contains positive thoughts from the Sheikh and good news about Dubai. And there *are* good things, for instance the progressive steps taken by the country's leadership to address socially relevant issues like consanguinous marriages and the increasing number of children born with genetic abnormalities, the problems of single women, divorces, the pressing issue of preserving national identity, and so on.

The UAE is governed by Sharia Law, which lays down the rules and regulations for various things including the media. There are two indigenous telecom companies, Etisalat and Du, both of which have on their list a number of sites that are inaccessible in the UAE. The social networking site Orkut, for instance, may not be viewed in the country. And what is interesting is the way that it is censored. A cartoon of a veiled Emirati grandmother (a figure from the Freej series by Emirati cartoonist Mohammed Saaed Harib) adorns the page. A polite reminder to the viewer that his/her intention to access that particular page doesn't go down well with *her*, it is both outrageous and funny.

Even with the best of intentions, a working journalist will find him- or herself becoming an "other", a construction, shaped by social, cultural and political pressures from the environment in which they work. And when you see this happening to yourself, you simultaneously become aware of how easily we do this to those that we encounter—we make them "other".

References

"Ageism." In: *Online Etymology Dictionary*. Ed Douglas Harper. Website, <http://www.etymonline.com/index.php?searc h=ageism&searchmode=none>

"Communications in the United Arab Emirates." In: *Wikipedia*. Website, <http://en.wikipedia.org/wiki/ Communications_in_the_United_Arab_Emirates>

"Gulf News, the History of." In: *GulfNews.com*. Website, <http://gulfnews.com/about-gulf-news/help/the-history-of-gulf-news-1.446035>

Joyce, Miriam. "On the Road towards Unity: The Trucial States from a British Perspective, 1960-66." In: *Middle Eastern Studies*, 35, 2, April 1999, 45-60.

Key, Wilson Bryan Key. *Subliminal Seduction*. New York: Signet, 1974.

Khaleej Times Online. Website, <http://www.khaleejtimes. com/aboutus.asp>

Molis, Debbie. "Definition: Subliminal Perception." In: *SelfGrowth.com*. Website, <http://www.selfgrowth.com/articles/Definition_Subliminal_Perception.html>

Monck, Adrian. "The Origins of 'Churnalism'." In: *Adrian*

Monck: A Blog about News, May 18th, 2008. Website, <http://adrianmonck.com/2008/05/the-origins-of-churnalism>

National, The. Website, <http://www.thenational.ae/about-us>

Ramanan, Manju. *Golden Tribute*. Dubai: Sterling Publications, 2009. Online version, <http://issuu.com/bbrdubai/docs/goldern_tribute>

NOTE: The Indian examples cited are from my professional experience working for the *Times of India Daily* in India as well as for *Femina* magazine (which is now a collaboration between the *Times of India* and the BBC). The views expressed are my own, and there is no intention of tarnishing or harming the reputation of either of these publications.

ENCOUNTERING THE OTHER

THE IMAGE OF GERMANY AND ENGLAND IN THE NEW MEDIA IN BULGARIA—NEW STRATEGIES OF DEVELOPMENT IN THE PRINT MEDIA

by DETELINA METZ & MADELEINE DANOVA

THE MASS MEDIA are undoubtedly the

> major cultural and ideological force standing in a
> dominant position with respect to the way in which
> social relations and political problems are defined and
> the production and transformation of popular ideolo-
> gies in the audience addressed (Hall 1988, 118).

In this sense media discourse is often viewed as being in inter-
mediate relation to ideology and power in society. The enor-
mous influence of the mass media in defining a group's place
in society in the age of nationalism has also received a lot of
critical attention. Benedict Anderson (1991), for example, has
argued that it is print-languages that have laid the foundations
of national consciousness (44) and that one of the most vivid
epitomes of the secular, historically clocked, imagined community of the Nation is the newspaper (35).

The newspaper as the technical means for "re-presenting" the Nation, however, poses the question of how the space of the national has been changed under the forces of globalization and the "loss of identity" that Julia Kristeva (1986) talks about, which have substituted for the horizontal, homogeneous empty time of the Nation's narrative the pluralism of the national sign, where difference returns as the same to question the solidity and to re-negotiate the *chronotope* of the Nation. (The term chronotope is used here in the sense suggested by Holquist's critical re-reading of Bakhtin (Holquist 1990) and is viewed as a particular combination of time, space and value as has resulted in historically manifested narrative form characterized by the simultaneity and inseparability of its elements.)

Thus, mass media discourse as studied by us has been assumed to have all the necessary characteristics of a cultural phenomenon able to produce and re-produce meanings and ideologies and not serve only as an "indicator" or a "stimulus" of the social and cultural processes in society. That has made it possible to interpret it within the framework of a more general philosophy concerned with the way the Other is constructed, such as the one proposed by Mikhail Bakhtin.

The present study has tried to find all the articles in one of the "new media" newspapers in Bulgaria, *Dnevnik*, about Germany and England (we talk about "England", not "the United Kingdom"—in popular discourse in Bulgaria the latter term is seldom used—but readers should please imagine the inverted commas!), especially those related to their attitude to Bulgarian accession to the European Union, for seven months before it became a fact on January 1st, 2007, and ten months afterwards, a period long enough to allow useful generalizations and conclusions with regard to the image of the Other.

A special task of the paper has also been to see if that image has changed along with the Bulgarian print media writing practices during these political transformations. The issues examined cover the period from June 2006 to October 2007. The textual corpus consists of 107 articles dealing with Germany (both domestic and bilateral relations, for the whole period of study) and 102 dealing with England (for the period July 2006 to June 2007).

The analysis of the gathered material has been done on the basis of discourse analysis since, in order to be able to see it in the light of a more general philosophy concerned with the image of the Other, it is necessary to use an analytic method that will reveal the content of the media message. We have therefore turned to media content analysis as developed by George Gerbner (1985) as an objective method of quantitative description of the texts under analysis. This type of analysis is focused on extracting from mass media discourse such elements as *existence*, *importance*, *value*, and *relationship*, *i.e.*, it deals with the basic elements of discourse such as thematic structure, propositional nature, characterization and action structure, social typing, and so on.

Inquiring into all the elements and comparing the results from the two surveys has made it possible to proceed with the qualitative analysis of these messages in the terms proposed. The four dimensions of *existence* (What is?), *priorities* (What is important?), *values* (What is right or wrong, good or bad, *etc.*?) and *relationships* (What is related to what, and how?) deal respectively with such terms and measures of analysis as *attention* (prevalence, rate, complexity, variations), with the questions: What is available for public attention? How much and how frequently?; *emphasis* (ordering, ranking, scaling for prominence, centrality or intensity), with the question: In what context or order of importance?; *tendency* (measures of critical and differential tendency, qualities, traits), with the question: In what light, from what point of view, with what associated judgements?; and *structure* (correlations, clustering, structure of action), with the question: In what overall proximal, logical, or causal structure? The analysis has taken into account not only the written materials, but also the photos, and the various fonts and graphic styles employed, as well as the place where each of the texts appears.

Before we proceed with the actual analysis of the data obtained, it is important to look at the way the print media have changed in the last few decades.

The Daily—Old-Timer or New Medium?

IT HAS ALWAYS been difficult to give a comprehensive picture of the world as it is. If you decide to walk around in the "thick forest" of the Bulgarian press today, you will be surprised by the multi-colored hustle and bustle there. After the barren desert of the media in Bulgaria during the years of the communist regime, a new epoch in media development began with the fall of the Berlin Wall, in the direction of aggressiveness and sensationalism, with the distinction between the serious and the tabloid press often quite blurred. Since the mid-Nineties, however, a new phenomenon has begun to develop, namely the emergence of so-called "new media" which presuppose a new way of communicating. It is no longer sufficient for the modern newspaper merely to be sensational. It has become necessary to seek new flexible models for attracting the readers' attention and interest. The most characteristic features of the new media can be seen at first glance—the many photos, colored and large-scale, statistical graphics and the so-called "visual statistics", colored headlines, different fonts, the pages designed much more spatially. The people who have introduced this modern style into the press explain the unusual design in terms of a change in the communicative goals of the newspapers—according to them, the readers should be helped in their attempts to extract the information they need as quickly as possible. The in-depth feature articles meant for the "serious" reader have given place to new hybrid genres of media texts, able to satisfy a customer who is always in a hurry. Thus a new form of reception has emerged, called "scanning", where the reader, looking for key-words and phrases, becomes a "scanning reader".

Contemporary audiences are very much open to innovations, while cyber space additionally stimulates the search for novelty.

And if two decades earlier it was enough to rely on the aesthetics of visual representation, *i.e.*, on text, photo and white-space distribution and the use of color, today it is not the graphically well executed presentation that is the sign of professionalism and quality, but rather the rhetorically well-arranged works where the *design* is of the utmost importance for the readers' orientation, selection, information-gathering and reception. The language of the news has always sought to be precise and authentic. But yesterday's question of what language to use in order to carry out a successful communication between reader and author sounds quite different today: How to present information to the scanning reader?

Time—the Real Rival of the Newspaper

THE OVERWHELMING MASS of information on the one hand and the less and less time that readers today have for the print media on the other have led to diverse on-line versions so that the interest of young readers in particular can be aroused. What is the attitude of the so-called iPod generation? They expect the paper to be small in size, so that it can be scanned and read easily, that it be terse, compact and clear. Only attractive, reader-oriented interactive media can keep the attention of the new reader. One of the major transformations in the sphere of the print media has been the reduction in the size of most of them. After 2003, when the British *Independent* started to offer two versions of the newspaper—the traditional broadsheet and an experimental compact version—which led to a market boom *against* a trend of falling newspaper sales, even *The Times* decided to abandon its 200-year broadsheet history and choose the tabloid format. This format does not mean a smaller body of newspaper material. It is accompanied by new concepts in writing and the offering of information: reduced length of news and features, combined with constant updates. The newspaper of the new generation carries mainly short overseas business news and the current figures from the stock market.

Modern Design—the Journalistic "Know-how" of the Print Media in the Twenty-First Century

JUST AS IN earlier times, the task of journalists remains that of informing their readers using codes that will be comprehensible to all concerned. In the new millennium the print media have come closer to the type of communication that we have on the Internet. The print press has become not only visually more informative but there has been a process of creating clusters of information on particular topics. This modular design creates the possibility of selective use. Along with the traditional means of creating coherence, the practice of highlighted quotes has been introduced, which attracts the reader's attention and makes it possible to keep this attention longer. Thus, stylistic and visual representations blend, and the concept of design comes to integrate form and content, as well as visualization and formulating of ideas. There is an internationalization of visual stylistic devices as far as contemporary newspaper design is concerned.

There has been a rediscovery in the print media of the impact of the white spaces on the page. After the saturation of the audience with color information, a new visual print culture can be observed: contrast formatting, large black-and-white photos, and texts which immediately attract the reader's attention.

In this struggle to keep the oldest mass media alive there is a new ally, the "audio newspaper" or so-called "podcasting" newspaper, which includes not only recordings of the newspaper articles but specifically created articles which the readers can listen to whenever it is most convenient for them. Like such newspapers as the *San Francisco Chronicle*, *Die Zeit*, and the *Hamburger Abendblatt*, the Bulgarian *Dnevnik* (*Diary/Journal*) publishes asynchronic radio news in digital format.

One of the most important features of contemporary mass communications is their *individualization*. The way that the contemporary press combines print copy with interactive online broadcasting and the distribution of an E-paper is part of this tendency to guarantee to the audience the right to choose what, when, where and how much to read.

The E-Paper Euphoria

BESIDES THE WELL-KNOWN channels of information—print, online, mobile—another form is now being used in the struggle for survival of the newspaper, *i.e.*, the E-paper. In Europe and the USA this term designates the electronic version of the newspaper. Many of the most respected newspapers in the world have their E-paper versions, for example, *The Times, The New York Times, The Observer, The Washington Post, Die Presse,* the *Handelsblat,* the *Frankfurter Allgemeine Zeitung, Le Monde,* and so on.

Dnevnik is the first Bulgarian newspaper to use this relatively new hybrid form (from mid-2006) to distribute its printed version. A one-to-one correspondence version of the print copy is published online, using the new opportunities for navigation and archive search of information. The reader gets access to this "paperless paper" at the moment of its print publication and in the same format, which is however enriched by the endless opportunities offered by the Internet, such as quick access from any point worldwide, the choice of reading it online or offline, and a guaranteed update of the information. Moreover, the E-paper can be received via RSS (*Really Simple Syndication,* a version based on the hmt-format, which serves for the exchange of news and other information on the web) before the print version is distributed.

The E-paper has other advantages too, such as:

Quick and easy navigation

A way of selecting items at the very beginning, arranging the pages which are of interest to the particular reader and eliminating the rest

> Quick, cheap and sure delivery at the moment of pub-
> lication

The E-paper is a medium that combines the advantages of print and online media, blending the models of the print and online newspapers. The tendency to select only the information needed leads inevitably to the use of online features such as multimedia presentation, hyper-textuality, and interactivity.

The Newspaper *Dnevnik* as a Modern New Medium in Bulgaria

IN OUR OPINION, *Dnevnik* is the best example of the new interactive media in Bulgaria. Its first issue was published in 2001, which means that it is not burdened by the political heritage of communism.

Contemporary European culture is distinguished by a certain uniformity of newspaper design concepts, and *Dnevnik* is no exception. It is a business-oriented daily, which appears from Monday to Friday (European data show that there has been a drop in the number of newspaper copies sold on weekends in the last few years). Till 2005 the newspaper was published as a broadsheet and was the last of the Bulgarian newspapers to use this format. After a careful survey of reader preferences, the newspaper adopted the so called tabloid format—smaller, more compact and easier to read.

The editorial policy of the newspaper is oriented towards liberalism: less state control, and more business initiatives and freedom. The German publishing group Georg von Holtzbrinck GmbH, which also publishes the German newspaper *Handelsblatt*, had a fifty per cent stake in the Economedia publishing group until November 2007, when the Bulgarian owners acquired all the capital.

Dnevnik is a basic and significant source of information for decision-makers because of its comprehensive business section. According to recent research data, *Dnevnik* is the daily with the largest number of corporate subscribers, reaching over 9,000 companies. The overall reach of the newspaper is estimated at over 51,000 people every day, not counting the readers of the full on-line version of the newspaper, which has about 50,000 identified visitors every day. The website provides free archive access to the printed issues. A big advantage of the medium is that during the day the official website is regularly updated with the latest news.

People who choose to read *Dnevnik* are mainly economically active people. According to a survey by Economedia in March 2009, 76 per cent of the readers of www.dnevnik.bg are aged between 18 and 45, and 56 per cent have a university degree, compared to the national average of 14 per cent.

Seventy journalists work for the newspaper, making it the largest newspaper team in Bulgaria.

A very important aspect of this newspaper is its forum, where readers can express their own opinions and views, which makes it interactive and gives them a real opportunity to participate in the making of the news. The influence of global trends in the newspaper industry has marked *Dnevnik* as well. It is oriented entirely towards the selective reader who needs quick and objective information. The visually enriched newspaper is therefore full of "visual statistics".

European themes are of great importance, and comprehensive use is made of the opportunities offered by the international news and info-stats exchange. The newspaper makes abundant use of the rediscovered "white spaces" and has managed to remain untouched by the aggressive colorfulness of the other Bulgarian papers. It thus directs the readers' attention very successfully towards the *content* of the news pieces, which aim at precision and objectivity. It seems to us that the journalists at *Dnevnik* subscribe to the three most important rules of objectivity:

Rule 1: Facts should be precise
Rule 2: News should present all points of view

Rule 3: News should not contain any form of comment

For any newspaper, its sources of information are of utmost importance. They must be authentic and clearly indicated. *Dnevnik* quite often quotes Reuters, Spiegel-Online, the *Guardian,* the *Financial Times*, or the *International Herald Tribune.*

The selection of news is the most important issue for any newspaper. The news profile of *Dnevnik* is clear-cut—news about the European Union, and about foreign and domestic policies, especially those concerning business and education—and in line with the well-established taxonomy of types of news, namely:

A. News that *must* be reported—news of great importance for the audience, usually the leading news on the front page
B. News that *should* be reported—news that is of interest to many readers, who expect to be told what the outcome is
C. News that *might* be reported—news that entertains without negative impact, all the news discussed here being from types A and B

News in *Dnevnik*

LANGUAGE IS USED not simply in direct human communication, it makes possible relations between man and the world and *vice versa.* The language of the news has all the features of a specialized jargon, in between technical and everyday speech. It has been created by the necessity to present complex themes objectively. Unlike all other specialized languages, this one needs to be understood by the general public. Following the separation of news from commentary after 1945 and the revolution in newspaper design in the Seventies, the news, the report, the commentary and the feature remain the most important genres in print journalism. The new needs of the reader, however, entail new methods of presenting the news today:

1. Analysis, mixing news with commentary in some combination
2. Using different stylistic devices to "fill in" a generic news format

The news is the most concentrated of the generic formats in journalism. In a pluralistic society, the existence of well-researched, authentic and diverse news is the basis for what politicians call "democratic education of the will".

But what makes news valuable? The most important points are that the information is

> meaningful
> current
> concentrated, but easy to understand
> offered without any comments
> interesting to the readers

As far as the language of the news is concerned, it should be terse and should present the most important facts. This is valid for so-called "hard news", although due to media competition the distinction between "hard" and "soft" news is becoming more and more blurred nowadays. The result is the creation of new hybrid forms of news. From the great variety that exist, here are the ones most often used by *Dnevnik*:

A. Primarily informative texts, in which the very headline gives the most important information to the reader
B. Persuasive texts, with a clearly expressed opinion. The major goal of these texts is to arrange the information according to the value system of the author
C. Bifocal texts, the best example of which is the interview structured on the alternation of questions and answers

The Image of Germany and England in *Dnevnik*

THE MAIN TYPE of article found in the process of research was the news report, but there were commentaries, features, editorials and interviews as well. To classify the articles about Germany we used the categories of the E-newspaper: *News*, *Europe*, *Markets*, and *Sports*, the first two naturally falling within the area of our research, as well as the dimensions offered by Gerbner for the articles about England from the print version, our aim being to survey the way in which the image of the Other has been constructed within the national discourse in Bulgaria at a time of shifting national values.

In the first category, News, we found a lot of articles connected both with the domestic and the foreign policies of Germany and England, but also articles about important business events and trends.

In the second one, Europe, the news is entirely devoted to the European Union, its policies and economy. Interestingly enough, one of the major topics for the journalists of *Dnevnik* is that of climate change. A large percentage of the articles dealing with Germany are about education, which has always been a priority in Bulgarian society. The most important political events, accompanied by appropriate photos, are also well-reported. Only after Bulgaria's accession to the European Union does the number of articles concerned with major cultural events start to become dominant. It is important to note that the boundaries of the two categories News and Europe quite often seem to fluctuate, which is understandable given the fact that Europe and the European Union are now of the utmost importance for Bulgaria (as part of both of them). But the interest in Europe rises with the accession, articles on European topics in 2006 representing 46 per cent of all articles about Germany, whereas in 2007 this becomes 50.9 per cent.

The articles from the print version dealing with England show the same tendency, although they also present some other major problems arising out of the interrelation between national

Self and foreign Other, as a sample for September 2006 shows. The major issue is the closed labor market in England and the feeling among Bulgarians and Romanians that they are being treated as second-class citizens. (In Germany, there have been no such problems and migration has primarily been connected with education.) Out of the 27 articles which talk about England, ten are devoted to the issues of labor migration. Quite untypically for *Dnevnik*, there is even an article which casts objectivity aside and uses irony and sarcasm in describing the policy of the British government ("Rulgars will not come", from the September 26th, 2006, issue, "Rulgars" being a humorous coinage for "Bulgarians and Romanians").

Moreover, there is a whole page with three articles under one headline. "The British Melting Pot", in the September 1st, 2006, issue which specifically takes up the question of the Nation and the Other viewed through the doctrine of the homogenizing forces operating within the field of the national. The articles translated from foreign newspapers give basic facts and figures regarding the immigrant labor force in the European Union, but the graphic design suggests a different note, one of dissatisfaction and even irony about the attempts of the British government to preserve "national purity", after it became the main target of this dissatisfaction. (Unfortunately, we cannot reproduce the page here, but it is also a very good example of the novel use of "white spaces" in the new media of today.)

Such examples obviously require human behavior to be seen as being derived from the use humans make of language, based on the assumption that language plays a special role in a universe that can be conceived as an endless *semiosis*. The way in which identity is linked to epistemology and language has always been an acute problem of philosophy. What interests us more, however, is the relation between the Self (in this case the collective self of the group) and the Other in the light of *dialogism*, an approach exemplified in the writings of Mikhail Bakhtin.

The main reason for choosing this approach is less that it is an attempt to grasp human existence through language, than the fact that it places a distinct emphasis on the central role of the *dialogical nature* of language. Dialogue is viewed as a manifold phenomenon comprised of an utterance, a reply, and the relation between them. Thus existence for Bakhtin is both an event and an utterance, *i.e.*, a dialogue that is carried on at each level by different means, the most powerful being language. In this way the Self will never have an absolute meaning in itself because as a sign, like the words in language that segment experience into meaningful patterns and thus register difference, the Self's ultimate characteristic is in being what the Other is not. And as such, it will always remain asymmetrically dual, dependent for its existence on the Other. In fact, the Self is not only dependent on the Other but is in relation with it, a relation that is an essential part of its being. In this sense the Self is not even a duality but, at the very least, a triad consisting of a center, a not-center and the relation between them. This relation is metaphorically represented by Bakhtin as *dialogue*, the simultaneous unity of differences in the event of utterance, much like the *dialogical* identification of the subject in cultural discourse proposed by Homi K. Bhabha (1990).

Besides, the Self/Other relation should be conceived, according to Bakhtin, not as a dialectical either/or but rather as the different degrees to which each possesses the Other's Otherness. Obviously, since the identification is always constituted through the Other, it is an endless process of substitution, displacement or projection. In other words, if we endeavor to "know" the Nation as an entity we have, if we follow Bakhtin's dialogical epistemology, to put it into a relation of simultaneity with something else. On the other hand, that simultaneity of the Self and the Other is a much-contested space and the only way by which it can be mediated is by politics, *i.e.*, by negotiating between the value systems of the two entities involved. This is because, first and foremost, Bakhtin's dialogism conceives of being as an event and of human beings as a project or a deed, the deed of having constantly to make judgements.

The fact that Bakhtin puts so much stress on Otherness and above all on Otherness as *other values* means that one of the most important actors for him is community—which turns dialogism into a particular kind of social theory. This means that the Other is always perceived in socially and historically specified categories, since nothing can be perceived except against the perspective of something else.

The background against which every figure can be seen may vary—for literature, Bakhtin suggests that genre is the pattern against which perception of any particular text at any particular time allows us to see it as distinct. In the case of society we suggest that one of the possible patterns is the *ethnie*, in the sense suggested by Anthony D. Smith (1991). It will be of the same order as a self, a story, a genre, *i.e.*, like the various disguises that the invariant norm takes throughout Bakhtin's philosophy. The individual variables which are not only perceived against this normative background but also distort it also come under various disguises: an Other, a plot, a specific chronotope or, as in our case, the Nation. And as the Other permits the Self, as the plot permits the story, so the Nation permits the ethnie. The fixative power of such categories is in fact what enables sense to be made out of the flux of experience. But the systematic claims to stability can never exist as a given, they must always be made up, conceived or, to use Benedict Anderson's word, "imagined".

It should be clear then that such a view of human existence will presuppose constant striving to stop the flux of experience, to resolve Bhabha's "perplexity of living", to articulate Bakhtin's heteroglosia of the world—and the way humans try to do this within the sea of ethnic differences is to invent the Nation. But once invented, it needs the Other for its own self-realization, for "uttering" its own existence in order to make it real.

The fact that existence can be defined as an event of utterance makes it possible to investigate how identity is constructed through language, though language viewed as action/relation in context, *i.e.*, as a discourse which does not merely reflect a situation but is a situation in itself. It is in this sense that the nation can be viewed as a "narration" containing the different stories of the selves comprising it which split its "modernity" into the ethnography of its culture's contemporaneity, in Homi K. Bhabha's words (1990), and render the nation-space not as homogenized stasis but as something that is in the process of articulation. This is the only way not only to establish the cultural boundaries of the nation but all those thresholds of meaning that Bhabha speaks of, which must be crossed, erased, and translated in the process of cultural production. Thus the totalizing and differentiating forces of language as used in a particular social context in a dialogical exchange can account for the ambivalent, Janus-faced, discourse within nation-space. This view of the nation also permits the use of discourse analysis as a tool for uncovering the way the split of Self and Other is realized within the boundaries of the national culture and within the discursive field of the new print media.

References

Anderson, Benedict. *Imagined Communities*: Reflections on the Origin and Spread of Nationalism (1983). Second edition. London: Verso, 1991.

Bakhtin, Mikhail. *Speech Genres and Other Late Essays.* Ed. Caryl Emerson / Michael Holquist, transl. Vern W. McGee. Austin, TX: University of Texas Press, 1986.

Bhabha, Homi K. (Ed). *Nation and Narration*. London: Routledge, 1990.

Gerbner, George. "Mass Media Discourse: Message System Analysis as a Component of Cultural Indicators." In: *Discourse and Communication: New Approaches to the Analysis of Mass Media Discourse and Communication.* Ed. Teun A. van Dijk. Berlin: Walter de Gruyter, 1985, 13-25.

Hall, Stuart. *The Hard Road to Renewal: Thatcherism and the Crisis of the Left.* London: Verso, 1988.

Holquist, Michael. *Bakhtin and His World.* London: Routledge, 1990.

Kristeva, Julia. "A New Type of Intellectual: The Dissident." In: *The Kristeva Reader.* Ed. Toril Moi. Oxford: Blackwell, 1986.

Smith, Anthony. *National Identity.* Harmondsworth, Middx.: Penguin Books, 1991.

WORDS AND PHRASES

ENGLISH AND GERMAN PERSPECTIVES

by Hansjörg Bittner

Interviewing the linguist and field researcher Dan Everett, who is best known for his controversial analysis of the Pirahã language, Geoffrey Sampson (2009) made the following comparison:

> [Y]our recent writings gratuitously "exoticize" Pirahã, by describing morphologically complex words with simple meanings in terms of the etymological sense of the roots—as if a Frenchman were to argue that English-speakers have a weird view of intellectual activity, because instead of the simple concept *comprendre* they say that people *se tiennent debout sous* (understand) an idea (220 f.).

Not quite as exotic will be the comparative analysis in this essay of the different points of view revealed by some words or phrases in English and German—words or phrases which have been randomly selected to shed light on their respective modes of constructing meaning. The examples do not aspire to linguistic exaltation, but are intended as reminders of the playfulness inherent in language: and they can be said to have served their purpose, if their explanations make you smile, at least occasionally.

No matter whether the factual evidence supports a semantic analysis based on the not-too-serious disassembly of a compound or phrase, the conclusion, albeit logical in itself, often turns out to be as flimsy as it is ludicrous. Take, for instance, petrol consumption. A car in Britain would have a mileage of, say, 53.3 miles per gallon; in Germany, the same car would use 5.3 litres per hundred kilometers. Whether you look at petrol consumption in terms of miles per gallon or in terms of litres per hundred kilometers—each perspective betrays a different business attitude. Whereas the Germans would seem to set a target and then invest whatever is required to achieve it ("Let's see how much petrol we need to do a hundred-kilometer trip"), the British and Americans draw up a budget and try to make the most of it ("Let's see how far we get on one gallon"). Any real-life confirmation of such wisdom, though, would be accidental.

Whether accidents are also accidental is a moot point. Some of them are caused by what Americans most sensibly call "driving while intoxicated" or "DWI" (if they feel intimidated by the onslaught of eight syllables). The situation referred to is obvious: a person under the toxic influence of alcohol is driving something (most likely: a vehicle, less likely: someone crazy, and certainly not: a nail into the wall). Note that all that an intoxicated driver is supposed to be doing is—driving. In Britain, however, intoxicated drivers are more daring because they "drink and drive", just as other people might prefer to drink and talk or drink and enjoy. While not compulsory, the possible simultaneity of drinking and driving is at least highly sugges-tive, conjuring up the image of a driver with a good many cans of lager on the bar-like dashboard top of his or her vehicle. In Germany, these cans of lager might be literally found sitting in the driver's seat, because here the phrase in question is *Alkohol am Steuer* (*i.e.*, "alcohol behind the steering wheel", compare *Frau am Steuer*).

The question whether the Germans or the British are better at holding their drink cannot easily be answered. Certainly that most popular pastime, pub-crawling—notably indulged in by students who go from one pub to the next to drink their fill—yields but little insight into people's capacity for alcohol. It would seem that a pub *crawl* could hardly involve a very lively round of the local public houses, no doubt due to the intoxicating effect of the alcohol. In Germany, on the other hand, a *Kneipentour* ("pub tour") or a *Sauftour* ("drinking tour") sounds like a much more attractive way of progressing from one pub to another. However, to conclude from this that a German is more likely to drink a Brit under the table than *vice versa* would be a mistake. For there are also British people who go "bar hopping".

Another aspect associated with alcohol is addiction, and so we come to the term "workaholic". Coined apparently by Wayne E. Oates in 1968 (see Safire 2000), the word was oxymoronically intended as a "serious jest" (Oates, 16). While referring in most cases to the danger of workaholism as a disease (as is evident from websites such as www.workaholics-anonymous.org), the term is also used in a playful and even positive way, as in: "President-elect Barack Obama's pick for Treasury secretary is relatively young, largely unknown and a proud workaholic" (Reddy 2008).

It is this potential to express a meaning that lies between jest and seriousness which has made the word (capitalized: "Workaholic") popular in the German language, too, despite the existence of the well-established German metaphor *Arbeitstier* (*i.e.*, "working animal"). With its connotations of mules and oxen, the German word cannot easily be positioned on the cline between positive and negative emotions. And as it also lacks the element of addiction, the ensuing gap is readily filled by the term "Workaholic".

While workaholism can relate to hard-working bunches of people in either Germany or England, there are other expressions that point to a somewhat better level of fitness among Germans. This is certainly true of sailors: the British simply *drop* anchor, whereas German sailors—strong as they are—*throw* it, the corresponding expression being *Anker werfen*. Fortunately, in many cases this task is performed by the ship, relieving British and German sailors of a heavy burden. A less weighty instance of the Germans getting more exercise than the British presents itself in the shape of the telephone. To respond to the ringing signal of this particular device, all a Brit has to do is to *answer* the phone. For Germans, this involves the use of one's legs, since in Germany what people do is "*go to the phone*" (the phrase being *ans Telefon gehen*).

Less suggestive of any nonsensical conclusions but interesting in terms of semantic optimization are the English word "screwdriver" and its German equivalent *Schraubenzieher*. While the first word is straightforward in the way it creates meaning (with the verb "drive" being defined as "bore"), the second ("screw-puller") is less obviously so, because screws are not normally *pulled*. This seems to be the reason why the term *Schraubendreher* ("screw turner")—not usually found in last-century reference books and still referred to as formal or technical by more recent dictionaries—is gradually establishing itself in everyday German as the correct signifier for a screwdriver.

A rather amusing difference in perspective emerges when we compare the expressions "lost property office" and *Fundbüro* ("find office"). While the German *Fundbüro* is apparently for people who have found something, the British or American lost property office would seem to welcome only those who have lost something. So someone who enquires at a lost property office in the United Kingdom whether his or her wallet has been found might almost expect to receive a negative answer, since the wallet in question will, of course, having been *found*, already have been taken to some *Fundbüro* in Germany. With increasing globalization and European integration, however, it would seem that officials in the English-speaking world have become aware of the problem, which they have now elegantly solved by creating the "lost and found (office)".

Stealing wallets is a crime, and people suspected of a crime may need an alibi, preferably a "cast-iron alibi". For German suspects, this alibi would have to be *hieb- und stichfest*, literally rendered as "blow- and stab-resistant". While the English alibi will definitely be satisfactory to a German, the German alibi may not be good enough for an English suspect. The reason for that is obvious: a cast-iron alibi is clearly also *hieb- und stichfest* (as any attempt to knock down or stab a cast-iron radiator will soon prove), but an alibi that is *hieb- und stichfest* will not necessarily be made of something as robust as cast iron. Whether an aluminum or even a stainless-steel alibi will do the trick is therefore a matter for the police to find out. As regards alibis, it is probably safer to specify the material that they're made of rather than their properties.

A man with a wife who is always telling him what to do and who will not tolerate any disagreement from him is referred to as a "henpecked husband" in English and as a *Pantoffelheld* ("slipper hero") in German. Compared with the disturbed rural idyll conjured up by the English phrase, the German term paints a more violent picture. The great *Deutsches Wörterbuch* (1854-1960) inaugurated by Jacob and Wilhelm Grimm defines *Pantoffelheld* as someone *der unterm Pantoffel steht* (part 13, column 1426)—that is, someone "who stands under the slipper". The image suggested here is that of a wife ready to hit her poor husband with a slipper. This would imply that the German *Pantoffelheld* is even worse off than his English counterpart.

Marriage might well become a dangerous situation to be in if the violent wife is wielding not a slipper but—a rolling pin. That wonderful kitchen tool is called a *Nudelholz* ("noodle wood") in German. The English term focuses on the tool's most important property ("rolling") and its purpose (to roll out pastry, dough, *etc.*), whereas the German word rather unspecifically refers to the (original) material of the tool and to its (original) application: it was a piece of wood used as a tool to make pasta. However, in a pejorative or jocular way, a *Nudel* can also refer to a person (usually a woman), which suggests the image of a wife brandishing the wooden tool as if it were a weapon. It could mean that German husbands are more likely to be hit with a *Nudelholz* than British husbands are with a rolling pin.

Violence is seldom the best method to achieve one's goal. More effective is a strategy that combines threats and cajolery, namely, that of "the carrot and the stick", or, in a German environment, that of *Zuckerbrot und Peitsche* (*i.e.*, "sweetmeat and whip"). While, according to the *Oxford English Dictionary*, the first known use of the English phrase dates from 1948, going back to "the proverbial method of tempting a donkey to move by dangling a carrot before it" (216), the German equivalent can be found as early as the 1870s (Wander 1867-1880). How, then, do the perspectives inherent in the two phrases differ? Both are metaphors for a wicked psychological persuasion technique; but while the English expression is linked to the world of animals, thereby distancing itself from its inherent wickedness, the German phrase uses archetypal images of *human* reward and punishment.

What is perceived as a punishment depends on the attitudes of the punisher and the punished. Thus, some people might even view the dark plugs of sebum in their facial hair follicles as a punishment, although there is no immediately obvious punisher. In German, these spots are called *Mitesser*—a word that literally (and with an alternative meaning) denotes "someone who eats together with you". The Grimms' *Deutsches Wörterbuch* suggests that both senses are, in fact, related: *man sah sie früher als den kindern angezauberte würmer an, die abmagerung bewirkten* (part 12, column 2343). In English: "they used to be regarded as worms magically engrained into children, causing them to become emaciated." That this belief is not restricted to the German perspective of the phenomenon might be inferred from the English equivalent "blackhead", which evidently relates to the black "heads" of the above worms. Such a view is supported by the etymology of the corresponding medical term "comedo": it goes back to Latin *comedere*, which means "to eat up, devour", and is "a name formerly given to worms which devour the body" (*OED*, 292). By comparison, the more common "blackhead"—a mere black spot—sounds rather harmless, even cute.

Other black spots are less innocuous, though, and particularly those in the realm of traffic. Thus, an accident black spot may be caused by black ice, *i.e.*, a thin layer of transparent ice, especially on a road surface. But how does the phrase "black ice" generate meaning? The most likely interpretation would be ice that looks black on tarmac or asphalt and which, therefore, is not easily noticed. That there are still other meanings that have nothing to do with ice on the road (American Meteorological Society 2000) need not concern us here. At any rate, the visual description inherent in "black ice" seems to be shared by the synonymous phrase "glare ice"—used in North America—since "glare" has been suggested to be etymologically connected with "glass" (*OED*, 676). Unlike the English expressions, the German equivalent, *Glatteis* (*i.e.*, "smooth ice" or, perhaps, "slippery ice"), makes sense more or less tautologically: the term implies that the ice has retained what are its proper natural properties, namely smoothness and slipperiness. Relating to traffic, the German word *Glatteis* signals danger more directly than the absence of color in the English phrase "black ice".

Color perception, or rather the precision of color names, yields another interesting difference in perspective between English and German terms. While traffic lights in Britain show red, amber, and green, in Germany they are said to display the colors *rot, gelb, grün* ("red, yellow, green"). But the true color of the light in the middle, however, is actually amber in Germany too. Referring to it as *gelb* instead of *bernsteinfarben* may be because the first of these color names is more convenient, being both shorter and commoner; yet it requires a brief process of abstraction on the part of the German road user. British road-users, on the other hand, are not required to be so imaginative because they are actually given the color they are mentally waiting for at the traffic lights.

Traffic is supposed to be fastest on the motorway. So how do you get there? Ideally, you can drive along a feeder road—preferably one without traffic lights. In Germany, you would take what is called a *Zubringerstrasse*, an *Autobahnzubringer* or simply a *Zubringer*. A boring matter-of-fact description, the German expression refers to a "road that brings (you) to the motorway". The English phrase, by comparison, is rather more telling, as a "feeder road" suggests a somewhat voracious motorway. To enter or leave a motorway, you use a slip road, that is, you slip into or out of the moving traffic, driving on an acceleration lane or a deceleration lane, as appropriate. Compared with "slip road", the German equivalents, *Auffahrt* and *Ausfahrt* (*i.e.*, "on-drive" and "off-drive"), are rather dull and unimaginative in their straightforwardness.

The ultimate purpose of a motorway is to save time. Yet such a benefit is of no avail if you oversleep and then miss an important appointment early in the morning. "Why didn't you set your alarm clock?" we might ask. And your answer would be: "I *did* set it, but the alarm didn't go off because the battery needs to be replaced." The solution is a mains-operated clock radio, *i.e.*, a combined radio and alarm clock. In standard compounding, the final nominal element reflects the basic meaning of the overall compound. Thus, a racing car is a car—one that is used for racing; and car racing is racing—with cars, not with horses. A clock radio is then, in principle, a radio: a radio with a clock. To infer that this clock is, in fact, an alarm clock, you may have carefully listened to the talkative salesperson in the shop or, alternatively, you may have had an enlightening experience with the wrongly pre-set clock radio bleating out its Starlight Express music at three in the morning. In Germany, the same gadget goes by the name of *Radiowecker* ("radio alarm clock"). This is then first of all an alarm clock, albeit one with a radio— German compounding rules being in this respect the same as English compounding rules. So, while the British buy their clock radio to listen to the radio and, occasionally, to find out what time it is, the Germans buy their *Radiowecker* with the intention of being woken up by whatever noise their integrated radio can produce at the time specified.

Getting up at the right time or arriving punctually for a

meeting might be fraught with unexpected problems—at least for a German in Britain or a Brit in Germany. If the meeting is scheduled for 10.30 a.m., the British participant might refer to that time as "half past ten" or, more colloquially, "half ten", whereas the German attendee would say *halb elf* ("half eleven"). It is obvious that this is going to cause confusion and misunderstanding. A German in Britain will likely arrive at the appointed place one hour early, a Brit in Germany one hour late. What do these different ways of telling the time show? The British, with their stirring history of kings and queens, tend to look back to the time that has passed ("a quarter past *ten*", "half past *ten*", though "a quarter to eleven"); the Germans, on the other hand, are less inclined to dwell on the past and, therefore, more forward-looking (*Viertel nach zehn*, *halb* elf, *Viertel vor* elf—"quarter past ten", but "half eleven" and "quarter before eleven"). This is even more so the case with those Germans, mainly from the east, who use a different system of telling the time: *viertel elf, halb elf, dreiviertel elf* (i.e., "quarter eleven", "half eleven", "three quarters eleven"). This pattern, difficult as it is for some West Germans to comprehend, follows a rather compelling logic: in the above example, it refers to a quarter, one half, and three quarters of the eleventh hour of the day.

Offering their customers everyday commodities at convenient opening hours and in a residential area—these are the characteristics of a convenience store, so called because it makes shopping convenient. In German, there is no such convenient term for the same phenomenon. This may have to do with the fact that, in Germany, the opening hours of shops are more tightly regulated than, for instance, in the United States. Another explanation might be that the rather comprehensive concept of "convenience" is not matched by a similarly useful term in German. Depending on the context, the options range from *Annehmlichkeit* (where something is "comfortable to use") to *Zweckmässigkeit* (where something is "appropriate for what is required"), with quite a few words and paraphrases in between. Accordingly, a convenience store might be a *Tankstellenladen* ("petrol station shop")—usually referred to as *Tankstelle*—or a *Tante-Emma-Laden* ("Aunt Emma shop"), one of those once outmoded and now re-emerging general stores that used to be the principal shopping destination before the advent of supermarkets and department stores. The convenience of the term "convenience", however, has not gone altogether unnoticed in Germany: convenience food is no longer covered exclusively by the plural form of the German term *Fertiggericht* (*i.e.*, "ready-made meal"), but, as a truly generic expression, *Conveniencefood* has now also found its way into German dictionaries.

Whether to buy convenience food or fresh fruit and vegetables calls for a decision. In the English-speaking world, a decision is made or taken. This implies that deciding something has to do with creativity (you "*make* a decision") or selection ("*taking* a decision" from several options that are available). In Germany, the decision-making process seems to be a more serious affair: as the expressions *eine Entscheidung treffen* ("hit a decision") and *eine Entscheidung fällen* ("fell a decision") suggest, Germans would either get a rifle and shoot at the decision-target, trying to *hit* it, or they would take an axe and *fell* the decision like a tree. Thus, while an English decision—beautifully created or carefully selected as it has been—is easily changed or reversed, a German decision can only be final, having been hit by a bullet or felled to the ground by the sharp blade of an axe.

German business people are then somewhat rougher and tougher than their British or American counterparts. This is also supported by the way in which creditors deal with their debtors. In Britain or the United States, the dunning procedure is followed by what is referred to as "debt collection". Having thoroughly intimidated the debtor with a spate of reminders, all a British or American creditor has to do is to collect the debt—a rather harmless course of action featuring a blandly smiling creditor and a meek and compliant debtor. German debtors, by contrast, appear to be more contrary and intractable, and the creditors have to exert some pressure if they want to get their money (the term in question is *Schuldeneintreibung*): here, the debt (*Schulden*) faces the same treatment that sheep face when they are driven (*Eintreibung*) into the pen.

The above list of differences in perspective between English and German words and phrases might be continued almost endlessly. Indeed, you can try it yourself—in English and/or German, or, for that matter, in some other language that you are familiar with: all that is needed is a keen eye and ear that spots any instances of funny or peculiar signification. The *banteranting* (to coin a term) in this paper will, I hope, have struck enough of a balance between sense and nonsense to encourage further interest in the *playfulness* of language.

References

American Meteorological Society. *Glossary of Meteorology.* Second edition. Cambridge, MA, 2000. Website, <http://amsglossary.allenpress.com/glossary/search?p=1&query=black+ice>

Grimm, Jacob / Grimm, Wilhelm. *Deutsches Wörterbuch.* 16 vols. [in 32 parts]. Leipzig: S. Hirzel, 1854-1960. Website, <http://germazope.uni-trier.de/Projects/WBB/woerterbuecher/woerterbuecher/dwb/wbgui>

Oates, Wayne E. "On Being a 'Workaholic'." In: *Pastoral Psychology,* 19, 8, October 1968, 16-20.

Reddy, Sudeep. "Who is Timothy Geithner?" In: *The Wall Street Journal,* November 21st, 2008. Website,<http://blogs.wsj.com/economics/2008/11/21/who-is-timothy-geithner/>

Safire, William. "The Lives They Lived: On Language; Wordplayers." In: *The New York Times,* January 2nd, 2000. Website, <http://www.nytimes.com/2000/01/02/magazine/the-lives-they-lived-on-language-wordplayers.html>

Sampson, Geoffrey. "An Interview with Dan Everett." In: *Language Complexity as an Evolving Variable.* Ed. Geoffrey Sampson / David Gil / Peter Trudgill. Oxford: Oxford University Press, 2009, 213-29.

Simpson, John A. / Weiner, Edmund S. C. (Eds.) *The Oxford*

English Dictionary: Second Edition (*OED*) (1989). Compact edition. Oxford: Oxford University Press, 1991.

Wander, Karl Friedrich Wilhelm (Ed.). *Deutsches Sprichwörter-Lexikon.* Leipzig: F. A. Brockhaus, 1867-80. Website, <http://www.zeno.org/Wander-1867/K/wander-1867-501-0616>

UNDERSTANDING THE OTHER

NEWS FROM THE PAST AND THE PRESENT

by Jesús Baigorri Jalón & Concepción Otero Moreno (Grupo Alfaqueque)

Introduction

EVEN A VERY simple comparative analysis of the past and the present shows that the coexistence of people (and peoples) of different cultures and languages has been a recurrent feature in the history of humankind. So, too, the presence of bilingual and bicultural persons who have facilitated—and continue to facilitate—communication among different people or groups. When we observe our present-day societies and we see that hospitals, courts, employment offices and police stations—but also hotels and tourist resorts—have to face the challenge of interlinguistic and intercultural communication on a daily basis, it is perhaps useful to look back and note that this situation is by no means exceptional and that solutions to those communication barriers have been found in different historical and geographical settings.

Migrations and transfers of population are as old as the human species, although every society—perhaps even every generation—may tend to think that they are experiencing this phenomenon for the first time in history. One of the elements involved in migration, particularly when migrants move across countries and languages, is the challenge of communication between the host society and the immigrants. Here, too, we see that certain people seem to be rediscovering the wheel every day, as if it were the first time that foreigners had arrived in a strange land where people spoke another language, and as if previous societies affected by the event had not developed the means to overcome that barrier in the past.

Our research team (*Grupo Alfaqueque*) has discovered a large number of instances, going back to the Middle Ages and to the time of the Spanish empire in the sixteenth and seventeenth centuries, in which explorers, members of religious orders and eventually representatives of the state found solutions to these problems of communication by establishing corps of interpreters and translators who mediated between local people, ignorant of the common language of the Spanish kingdoms, and the administration, for example in the courts (Baigorri / Alonso 2007; Alonso / Baigorri / Payàs 2008; Alonso / Payàs 2008; Grupo Alfaqueque 2010). Historical records, even those equivalent to our present-day press, such as chronicles, offer plenty of examples of that interaction and of a well-oiled system that had to deal with cases affecting territories as distant as Mexico, Peru or the Philippines, with a range of languages to dwarf many contemporary multilingual institutions. Looking back at the sixteenth and seventeenth century Spanish colonial empire, we see how its judicial system developed a set of sophisticated regulations in order to facilitate the hearings of people who did not understand Spanish. (And this applies to other colonial powers of that time, too. For instance, the first appointment of an official interpreter in New York City goes back to 1642—see the *New York Times (NYT)*, January 1st, 1899.)

With this in mind, we can perhaps take a fresh look at our apparently "sudden" and "unusual" problems of communication. If we approach the more contemporary situation of immigrants arriving in foreign countries from their own perspective instead of from that of the host authorities we will be in a better position to assess their needs and their feelings and to design appropriate, empathetic solutions. (It may sound strange to read, in the *NYT* for September 9th, 1900, a story about a French woman, accompanied by her child, who got lost in Manhattan and wandered the streets for a whole week, unable to find her husband, because no one could understand her French and she was thought to be a beggar. This happened in "cosmopolitan" New York City in 1900.)

IN THIS PAPER we are going to deal with two different sets of documents, which reflect different variables of time, countries, immigrant groups, languages and tradition. We will use press cuttings from American newspapers from the turn of the twentieth century, and news about Spanish immigrants in Germany from the Sixties and Seventies—with brief mentions of other nationalities in present-day Germany—from Spanish local media or from other newspapers, some of which were specifically published to meet the needs of emigrants abroad. We intend to show how the press can be used as a source to analyze linguistic and cultural mediation with regard to immigrants at different times and places. There has been previous research on the perception of immigrants by the press—see, for instance King / Wood (2001), Prieto Ramos (2004) and Igartua / Muñiz (2007)—but references to their communication difficulties and to the solutions found to solve these are comparatively scarce. In our paper we shall be looking at some references to obstacles to communication and how interpreters helped to overcome them, while remembering that journalists tend to omit the necessary presence of interpreters in exchanges that, otherwise, would be impossible, as if we lived in a pre-Tower of Babel paradise.

The United States at the turn of the twentieth century was populating immense territories—which belonged to Native Americans in pre-industrial times—and transforming the country into an urban industrial society thanks to the influx of waves of immigrants from different parts of the world. Those who supervised their arrival were, more often than not, recent immigrants themselves and were likely as a matter of course to view immigration with sympathetic eyes and with some awareness of the phenomenon. The normal process for a typical immigrant was to become American and to embrace the American way of life. That was then. Nowadays, issues such as the recent controversial legislation about immigrants in Arizona—with an obvious element of racial profiling—or the erection of new walls and fences to keep *them* away from *us* indicate that the matter is far from simple and far from being something of the past. Perhaps this shows that American society is *neither a melting pot nor a multicultural democracy* (Golash-Boza 2005, 750).

Postwar Germany is a different story. It was a country divided into two separate states under two different political regimes, both embarked upon the colossal endeavor of rebuilding their infrastructures, their factories and their respective social fabrics, which had been destroyed by the war that followed the years of Nazi domination and expansion. The western part, the Federal Republic of Germany, witnessed during the Sixties and Seventies what has been called the "German economic miracle", attributable to a series of factors, including the Marshall Plan and the presence of American troops in lieu of the German military, but also the hard labor of millions of workers from "the South", who were considered by the German government and people, at least at first, as "guest workers" *(Gastarbeiter* in German), that is, as people who would stay only temporarily and who would return to their countries of origin in an orderly manner, once the economic reconstruction effort was achieved (Limage 1985, 251).

This view completely ignored the realities of the social phenomena and the impossibility of establishing a "pure" culture—*all cultures are mixed ("hybrid", "cross-bred")* (Todorov 2008, 54)—despite the overwhelming evidence Germans had witnessed in their previous history. How many different cultures contributed to the societies that essentialists call "German", "French", or other mono-ethnic simplifications? (Hoerder 2005, 250). It seems, though, that the Germans were caught by surprise when they found themselves in the company of several million foreigners, who, with the passing of time, had children who grew up as Germans—with a little component of their parents' culture—and who spoke German like everybody else, but were often denied German nationality. Instead of the *jus solis* that prevails in the United States, Germany has a legal tradition of *jus sanguis*. Maybe this explains why we speak of "first-generation Americans" while in Germany it is common to see expressions such as "third-generation Turks".

> In the last two decades, historians have questioned societies' master narratives written under the nation-state paradigm. Scholars in the two North American societies, who had been socialized in the context of discourses about immigration, pluralism, and multi-culturalism, pioneered these new approaches. Scholars in several European countries have also turned to the many-cultured pasts of their societies. Their empirical data quickly revealed that the mono-cultural nation state was nothing but a fiction (Hoerder, 235).

But the different approaches still persist:

> While the rhetoric about being a "nation of immigrants" is strong in the United States, Canada and Australia, it is singularly absent in Europe. The view that European nations were constituted before mass immigration began is still dominant (Penninx *et al.* 2004, 2)

The two examples are a mirror image, not only because of the different approaches to immigration (comparing the two broad historical periods), but also because in the case of the United States we use the press of the country of arrival, whereas in the case of Germany we use mainly the press of the country of departure of the emigrants, that is, Spain. There is a big conceptual gap between the two: the American press is based on freedom of speech and is addressed mainly to a readership that is aware of the presence of their new fellow citizens, while the Spanish press under Franco was subject to the censorship of officially appointed civil servants and had a mainly propagandist aim. In both cases, however, it is good to read critically between the lines, because the media are never neutral and there is always a certain amount of manipulation involved.

The aims of this paper are: 1) to show in a few examples how the printed press—quite often the sole available record of the (oral) interpreted event—can be a source of information for the history of interpreting in its relation to migration, 2) to show that interpreters' profiles have been essentially multifaceted throughout history, concomitant to the diverse language needs and the variety of multilingual settings, 3) to illustrate some of the similarities between the past and the present as far as understanding the Other is concerned, 4) to show how those historical references can help us better understand our present-day societies, and 5) to encourage new research in this field.

1. Immigrants and the US Administration: Talking to Each Other (through an Interpreter)

THERE ARE HUNDREDS of references to language mediation through interpreters in the American press of the end of the nineteenth and beginning of the twentieth centuries. Those instances represent, however, an insignificant figure compared with the potential number of exchanges in which communication difficulties occurred. The topics of the news stories are extremely multifaceted and they tend to focus on individual cases rather than on the issue of interpreting in general. The reading of some of those articles gives us the idea that there is a need of mediators in order for the "Other" to communicate with the administration in an efficient manner. In this context, there is a coexistence of instances where a well-organized system of professional interpreters is in place and other cases where *ad hoc* responses seem to be the best available solution.

Using the theoretical approach of *framing*—Igartua / Muñiz (2007) have carried out extensive empirical research on the topic of immigrants and their perception by the Spanish press—we immediately see that the press tends to use references and schemata to allow the readership to understand the story. In the field of foreign languages and speakers we may conclude that the myth or the metaphor of the Tower of Babel—not necessarily in a literal manner—is present in many instances. So is the idea of the interpreter as a critical link, and of the polyglot, particularly if it is a child, as a marvel. We can infer from the American press at the turn of the twentieth century what everybody knows but tends to overlook: that American society was—and, of course, still is—multilingual and multicultural, and that the presence of bilingual individuals, often mere passers-by, was required for the daily dealings of citizens or visitors who were not fluent in English (with limited English proficiency, or "LEP" in more contemporary terminology) with the different branches of the administration. The first filter, symbolically represented by Ellis Island, was the immigration authorities, accompanied by a corps of interpreters, who were an instrumental cog between the newly arrived immigrants and the authorities that supervised their entry into the country.

We are going to use in this part of the paper just a few articles from two American newspapers—the *New York Times* (*NYT*) and the *Boston Daily Globe* (*BDG*)—from the late years of the nineteenth century and the first two decades of the twentieth century. The reasons for this choice are that this was a nation-building period, when a great number of immigrants—the "Other"—arrived to populate the United States, and that those newspapers have a long span in history and an easy electronic access. Our aim is to show only an exemplary illustration of a phenomenon that, let us say between 1880 and 1920, was of huge magnitude, with hundreds of thousands of newly arrived people who did not speak English, the official language of their host country. Linguistic and cultural barriers must have been an almost insurmountable obstacle to integration for the first generation of migrants, whose only luggage was quite often precisely their language(s) and customs. Also, it was a period of US history when the nation became an international power, with interactions beyond its political borders.

That the country was a mosaic of peoples and languages is shown by this announcement:

> The immigration service wants interpreters, and will receive applications for any of the following languages: Arabic, Armenian, Assyrian (Arabic), Bohemian, Bulgarian, Chinese, Croatian, Dalmatian, Danish, Dutch, Finnish, Flemish, French, German, Greek, Hebrew, Herzegovinian, Hindoo, Hungarian, Italian, Japanese, Lithuanian, Montenegrin, Magyar, Norwegian, Persian, Polish, Portuguese, Roumanian, Russian, Ruthenian, Servian, Slovak, Slovenian (Wendish), Slovenish (Kranish), Spanish, Swedish, Syrian, Syrian (Arabic), Turkish, Yiddish. There could be no better illustration of the diversity of American population (*BDG*, April 12th, 1907, 12).

It is interesting to note: 1) the great variety of languages and dialects in demand, 2) the fact that different branches of the administration (in this case, the immigration service) were competing for interpreters, an apparently scarce resource, and 3) that the aspirations of the immigration service were somewhat unclear. By calling for applications for interpreters, did the authorities assume that qualified interpreters were available for such an immense array of languages or simply that understanding and speaking the languages involved (English plus at least one of the others) was sufficient accreditation for the job? In other words, did they consider that interpreting skills were innate to any bilingual, no matter what age, gender, social class or education level? These are relevant questions, because today, one hundred years later, public opinion (and many authorities!)

in numerous countries continues to make the same assumption: you speak two languages *ergo* you are, naturally, able to translate and interpret.

We know that the recruitment of children as potential interpreters was a commonly used tool to overcome language barriers at the time of the encounter between European explorers and conquerors and pre-Columbian peoples in the American continent, and surely before then too (see, for example, Díaz del Castillo 1632, vol. I, 92, 94, and Karttunen 1994, 94). The hypothesis that children's brains easily adapt to learning foreign languages is well-established. It has always been—and it is still today—a common practice to use children as *ad hoc* interpreters, irrespective of the huge amount of evidence that discourages it! If anything, the examples we are presenting show that practice quite clearly. But another ingredient is added here: that of considering these cases as child prodigies, in these instances on account of their linguistic skills.

> [...] A little Mexican girl who arrived here six years ago from Mazatlan, being then 7 years of age, can speak Italian, French, and English fluently, and a little German, all picked up while romping with her playmates. This is but one in hundreds among the children, while among the elderly people there are scores who cannot speak a word of English, although some of them have lived in San Francisco for the past 10 and 20 years. They converse only in the language of their native land, and if any person speaking English addresses them, the children are called in as interpreters [...] ("Cosmopolitan San Francisco", in the *NYT*, August 13th, 1878, 2).

This text is a telling example of the cosmopolitan nature of late nineteenth century San Francisco, where only children seemed to be able to interpret seamlessly the symphony of languages that lay beneath the apparent cacophony of a Babel-like mosaic of neighborhoods. They were the big minds in tiny bodies who held a monopoly of communication.

In the following excerpt, a ten-year-old girl who arrives at the port of New York to join her father, in the company of other relatives in a process of family reunification, is, surprisingly for the journalist, able to speak five languages—and perhaps they overlooked that she probably also spoke Latvian, in view of her origin—in front of Ellis Island interpreters, who were supposedly familiarized with that type of linguistic marvel. This would be an example of language acquisition through a combination of private tutors—nothing peculiar for certain social classes in pre-Bolshevik Russia—and natural learning, although it may not be as easy to figure out how she could have learned the languages "naturally" than it is to predict that she will be able to learn English quite quickly. It seems easier to understand her acquisition of German—considering that Yiddish was the family language—and French than her learning of Italian, which was not so common in pre-Revolution Russia. The issue of *mastery* of those languages at such a young age would be more questionable, and should probably be understood as the ability to speak without an accent rather than as a full command of them. We can well imagine that she was able to speak in the languages briefly—busy Ellis Island interpreters would not have been able to spend hours testing the girl—and with a certain fluency. It is harder to believe that she would have been able to maintain conversations of a reasonable complexity for a ten-year-old child in all those tongues. That is, she would have been able to speak *in* five languages rather than five languages.

> [...] The girl's name is Minna Weisbeiner, and she came from Riga, Russia, with her mother, two little sisters and a brother. Her father is a prosperous tailor living at 83 Osborne st, Brooklyn. The family have come to join him.
>
> Minna attracted considerable attention and caused surprise at Ellis Island, where she conversed readily

with interpreters in Russian, German, French, Italian and Yiddish. She said she only went to school in Russia one year, but had private teachers part of the time and picked up the languages she had mastered herself. She has not acquired English as yet, but expects to do so in a little while, and says she hopes to go to school in America "for a number of years" ("In Five Languages: Little Russian Immigrant Girl Surprises Interpreters at Ellis Island. Is only 10 Years Old", in the *BDG*, December 15th, 1907, 7).

The last case we want to use in this section refers to a girl who acted as interpreter for her family. Speaking four languages was not *anything out of the ordinary*, according to this nine-year-old girl of Polish origin. What may seem odd to us is that the girl was called to act as interpreter in such a delicate situation as the threat of eviction of her family from their house in Lewinston (Maine).

> [...] The little girl usually acts as interpreter for the family, and it was in this capacity that she accompanied her mother to the office of the Lewiston police matron a few days ago, the family fearing eviction. The house in which they live was sold, and the new owner ordered them to move before Saturday in order that he might begin repairs.
> At the city building Frances explained the situation to the authorities—that the family would move as soon as they could find a tenement, but that they objected to being turned into the street, which they feared would be done.
> The city solicitor, William G. Tackaberry, explained the law in such cases. A day or two later, carpenters appeared at the house, saying they had come to make repairs. Mrs. Ozeckowicz, with Frances, hurried to the city building a second time, and were assured that

nothing which would prevent their living in the house could be done until the new owner had obtained a certain paper from the court (*BDG*, August 20th, 1922, 58).

This goes well beyond casual mediation in the street and reaches a point where an adult, a professional interpreter, should have been necessary, not least because it is quite unlikely that a nine-year-old child could understand the legal consequences of an eviction action, and because, if she did understand them, the emotional effect of being evicted would no doubt trigger an unjustified and unjustifiable level of stress in the child, with all the empathetic and affective involvement required to carry out the task. No English-speaking child would normally have been considered as suitable to receive that type of information from the authorities, let alone to act as a messenger between the authorities and their family. And yet we know, from numerous instances in the present-day printed press, that this is still a quite common phenomenon in the United States and in other advanced countries too, with children acting as interpreters for family members in medical, judicial and other contexts. For example: "We still see kids acting as the cultural brokers for their families, but it's no way to run a hospital" (Dr. Betancourt, director of multicultural education at Massachusetts General Hospital quoted in Anne Underwood / Jerry Adler, "When Cultures Clash", *Newsweek*, 145, 17, April 2005, 70).

We could multiply the number of examples of newspaper articles in which interpreters are mentioned. Ellis Island interpreters are one of the types (see, for instance, the *NYT* for April 7th, 1903, and for January 22nd, 1914). It is interesting to note that the place that for many years served as the clearing house for immigrants arriving at the America's eastern shore—indeed, a symbol for many Americans of European descent—had an interpretation service, with interpreters in uniform as linguistic assistants to the Immigration authorities (there is a photograph of an Ellis Island interpreter in uniform online at <http://www.gettyimages.es/detail/83931809/Hulton-Archive?language=es&location=ESP>).

A well-known person who acted as an interpreter at Ellis Island for three years (1907-10) was Fiorello Laguardia, the famous New York City mayor, who witnessed the frequent deportation of potential immigrants who supposedly suffered from different types of mental disorder. He contended that many of those cases were misdiagnosed due to communication problems or to the lack of medical skills to identify what the psychiatrist Joseba Achotegui from Barcelona described in 2002 as the "Ulysses syndrome", which presents one or several of the following symptoms: a feeling of being no-one, the pain of departure from one's own land and family, the melancholy of absence, an inferiority complex, the desire to return to an idealized childhood as a reaction to the hostility of a strange land, *etc.* One hundred years after Laguardia carried out his part-time job at Ellis Island we can still witness an influx of anonymous Ulysses, who continue to dream of no longer existing Ithacas and who find themselves entangled in the intricacies of being downgraded to the condition of strangers—of being "no one"—for their ignorance of the majority language. Many of them end up misdiagnosed with depression, although the real syndrome that they are suffering from is that of Ulysses, one of whose root causes is the language trauma (Achotegui 2009).

We shall finish this section by making brief reference to court interpreters, who appear quite often in the press articles we have used, particularly in cases where they were the main actors, either due to the demands of their job or because they broke the professional code of ethics. There is a great variety of types of interpreter in court settings, for instance, *general interpreter of the criminal courts*, *Supreme Court interpreter*, either of a county or a State, interpreters for the *Police Courts*, or for the *Court of Special Sessions* in New York City. And we find references to court interpreters in announcements of competitive exams (*NYT*, November 18th, 1897, "For a Court Interpreter"), of their appointments (*NYT*, May 8th, 1897,

"Brooklyn Interpreter Appointed"), their salaries (*NYT*, March 10th, 1875, "A Court Interpreter's Salary"), and even their obituaries (*NYT*, December 3rd, 1899, "Court Interpreter Dead"; *BDG*, May 21st, 1915, "Court Interpreter Dead"). But perhaps the most popular cases in the news are those which have to do with interpreters being used as scapegoats (*NYT*, April 12th, 1884, "The Interpreter Blamed") or breaching their code of ethics (*NYT*, July 2nd, 1888, "The Interpreter Explains"; *NYT*, October 12th, 1893, "Winked at His Chinese Interpreter"; *NYT*, December 14th, 1895, "An Interpreter Charges Bribery"; *NYT*, June 6th, 1896, "Court Interpreters At Odds"). What seems clear is that interpreting then—and now, as present-day news about interpreters in wars shows—was not an easy job.

> San Francisco, Cal., Dec. 1.—As indicative of the contempt manifested by the Chinese for the love of this country, Fou Sing, who has been acting interpreter between Port Surveyor Morton and bogus traders from China, sent word yesterday to the Collector that he was afraid any longer to perform his duties. His interpretations have been so faithful as to bring upon him the wrath of his countrymen who want the Chinese lauded as traders. They have hired "high binders" to shadow Fou Sing, who lives in momentary expectation of death (*NYT*, December 2nd, 1883, "Fears of a Chinese Interpreter").

This text raises the controversial issue of the professional code of ethics and impartiality of the interpreter. According to this article, the interpreter was faithful to language and to the San Francisco Port Surveyor but unfaithful to the expectations of his fellow Chinese citizens, to the extent that they were eager to kill him, a situation more reminiscent of interpreting in war zones than in presumably peaceful San Francisco. The interpreter, by performing his functions in a professional manner, runs the risk of ostracism in his own community—with the consequence of a forced migration elsewhere—while the majority group, in this case the American authorities, do not take the necessary steps to protect him with preventive measures before or during the interpreting event. In this instance, the mafia-like group of fake traders may have had the upper hand, but this was not always the case. In the famous Sacco and Vanzetti trial, interpreting difficulties were identified by several parties in the process due to the fact that the defendants spoke two different dialects and to a *conscious manipulation by a pro-prosecution interpreter.* This combination of circumstances *contributed to the swift guilty verdict handed down by the jury* (Carnevale 2009, 86), which was followed by the execution of the two anarchists.

In a historical study which compares criminal courtroom interpreting in eighteenth-century London with twenty-first-century Toronto, MacFarlane (2007) has shown that the use of "bystanders, jurors, and other witnesses [...] family members [...], character witnesses [...], co-defendants, jurors, or most disturbingly, the principal witness against the person requiring their services" as court interpreters (282)—a typical feature of eighteenth century London courts—is a practice that can and does still happen in our present-day society (an article published by the *Toronto Star* on October 4th, 2010, talks of the lack of accredited Mandarin interpreters in Toronto: "Grocer trial stalled over interpreter").

2. Contemporary Spanish Emigration to Germany and the Press

In 1964 the one-millionth foreign worker to arrive in Germany, a Portuguese called Armando Rodrígues, was warmly welcomed by local German authorities. All the media—the print media, television, radio, photographers—wanted to be there at Cologne central station when the immigrant arrived, to register such a memorable event, which was crowned with the generous gift of a *Vespa* motorcycle and several bouquets of flowers to the astonished Portuguese.

The more recent history of immigration has been followed and documented by the media, which deserve credit for having registered the ups and downs of the phenomenon, focusing their critical eye on certain aspects, assessing the achievements and the failures, the challenges and the positive effects, and last but not least disseminating the apparent "euphoria" that prevailed during the years of the German economic miracle.

Should we conclude that the story of the one-millionth foreign worker coincides with the upbeat mood of the moment? Or should we consider the event as an isolated instance, an exceptional piece of news lost in the middle of a far less euphoric and positive atmosphere? Unfortunately, this "less positive" environment reflects the reality that we more often find in the media, when they report on the Other, the foreigner, the immigrant, the Turk, the guest worker or a dozen other expressions used to designate a foreign citizen who lives in Germany. Exceptional or extraordinary success stories fall quite easily into oblivion. The ones that remain and have an impact on public opinion are precisely those that generalize without qualification or a minimum of reflection—as O'Reilly (2001) puts it, "[n]egative makes better news, and [a]lthough migration can be a positive thing, it is rarely viewed as such by the mass media, and there are not popular channels to correct the unbalanced view" (181 f.)—those that, so to speak, in foggy weather can spot the lost sheep in a thick forest, establishing absurd associations which sometimes reach, perhaps unwillingly, the level of racist opinions (Van Dijk 2003, 54).

In the Sixties these conceptual associations were linked with the constant use by the media of expressions that describe immigration and the temporary nature that it should have. The term *Gastarbeiter* ("guest worker"), used by politicians and by all the other people responsible in this matter, is the clearest evidence of that approach. The use of the term was a continuous reminder that foreign workers would stay only until the country reached a position in which it could do without them. At the same time, the media—particularly the popular press (and most notably the *Bildzeitung* daily newspaper, which in those days sold over 2.5 million copies—nowadays over 3 million—and had a readership way beyond that figure)—spread a distorted image of the foreign worker, with a considerable increase in the number of articles with stories about foreigners involved in violence and murder.

Even prestigious weeklies such as *Der Spiegel* spoke in 1964 of "a wave of foreign workers", of "an influx of immigrants heading for German salaries" ("Gastarbeiterschwemme", "Völkerwanderung zu deutschen Lohntüten", in *Der Spiegel*, October 7th, 1964, 44). In other sections, particularly in accident and crime reports, we find stories about sly foreigners who fool officials at the social welfare office in order to obtain benefits they are not entitled to, about cruel murderers coming from the South, criminal drug addicts and thieves, *etc.* This, in fact, is no news, since this kind of sensationalism—deplorable though it may be—is probably as old as the press itself. Yet readers of the press acquire, little by little, the idea that foreigners have higher levels of crime and delinquency than Germans, thus helping to consolidate totally unfounded prejudices and stereotypes.

In contemporary Spain we can also observe such phenomena in the media, particularly with the increasing number of immigrants arriving in the country—see Prieto Ramos (2004) and Igartua / Muñiz (2007). If a murder is reported in the accident and crime section of a newspaper, mention is made of the country of origin of the perpetrator: Colombian, Mexican, perhaps Russian. When reference is made to the mafia and organized crime, there is immediate mention of the origin of their members: Russians, Romanians, perhaps Albanians. But if a Spanish citizen from town *A* kills another Spanish citizen from town *B*, the information about the city of origin will be omitted, as irrelevant. Of course, the role of the media to inform us about everything and anything should not be questioned, but we should all be aware of the negative impact that a biased approach may have on the readership, creating prejudices and stereotypes that may eventually lead to social disturbances.

2.1 Spanish Emigration in the Spanish Local and National Press

Stories of economic boom, prosperity and job opportunities in Germany were echoed by the Spanish media. The echo was even more resounding, given that many young Spaniards were living in a precarious situation, characterized by a lack of well-remunerated jobs in a still mainly rural country, such as Spain was in the late Fifties. This may help explain the favorable reaction in Spain to the official initiative to recruit foreign workers to work in Germany and in other Central European countries.

From the end of the Fifties, different media, both at national and local level, launched a wide campaign of information on what was needed to be part of the legal emigration program to those countries. The campaign was encouraged—perhaps understandably, at a time when Franco's regime was trying to stabilize the country economically—by the *Instituto Nacional de Emigración* (National Institute of Emigration). In this context, it is curious to note the reiterated praise expressed with regard to the good work carried out by that institution, "whose aims are moved only by its encouragement to and protection of the Spanish worker" (*El Adelanto de Salamanca* (*AdS*), March 4th, 1961, 23), to quote, by way of one example from among many, one of the main daily newspapers from Salamanca that we analyzed for this research. In fact, with very few exceptions, the news relating to emigration found in that newspaper between 1959 and 1973, kept up a positive, even admiring, tone, particularly in the early years of that period. Thus we read that our workers "enjoy a good social, moral and cultural treatment" (*AdS*, October 18th, 1960, 7), their contracts include all kinds of guarantees, from the "payment of travel expenses, salary [...], social security" and even the "possibility of sending money to their relatives in Spain." Besides, according to that newspaper, some Spaniards feel so happy in Germany that "they express their appreciation to German companies [...] for their constant consideration towards them and for the opportunities they found to adapt in the best way possible to the labor environment" (*AdS*, April 27th, 1961, 3).

Once the euphoria of the early years is over, and although the press continues throughout the roughly two-decade emigration period to highlight the work of the Spanish authorities in the interests of emigrants, from the year 1961 the local press begins to echo the problems that Spanish emigrants have to face. First and foremost, there are the difficulties in finding decent and appropriate housing, with criticism expressed of the abusive behavior of landlords, who charge very high rents, of overcrowding, and of the lack of privacy in collective dormitories. The press also points out the difficulties with the language, which is considered as "an insurmountable barrier for the majority" (*AdS*, August 22nd, 1961, 5). From 1967 on, we can see in the local press, perhaps due to an initial awareness of the labor crisis which ended in 1973 with a halt in contracts for foreign workers (known in Germany as the *Anwerbestopp*: a halt to the recruitment of foreign workers in 1973 as a result of the oil crisis), that migration is considered "a human tragedy," "a sacrifice" (*AdS*, August 2nd, 1968, 7), a situation that can materialize in an "inferiority complex" which can lead to a "decrease in their own natural aptitudes" (*AdS*, December 24th, 1966, 4).

This pessimistic and discouraging tone does not change until well into the decade of the Seventies, which coincides with record figures, so far, of foreign tourists in Spain. Since this period corresponds to an important movement of returns of emigrants to Spain, the preoccupation expressed by the press is to create tangible incentives for those returned emigrants, taking advantage of the benefits they obtained in their stay abroad. Therefore, the sentimental and compassionate mood observed in the early years towards the emigrant turns into a different approach that highlights the numerous advantages derived from the emigration experience, which contributed to a personal improvement for many Spaniards and—with a clearly progressive hint—to the Europeanization of cultures (*AdS*, July 10th, 1971, 6).

La Región (*Diario La Región*, available in the archives for the dates 1966 to 1968), another press medium that we have analyzed, was a national-level publication aimed directly at Spanish citizens living abroad. Its tone and the points highlighted by this publication coincide with what we have observed in the local Spanish press, although we may add that, since *LR* was a newspaper which was sold in many places in Germany, France, Switzerland and the Netherlands, its approach was aimed in a more detailed manner at the problems and difficulties affecting workers and their families. In this context, the problems mentioned are not only those connected with housing or work, but also those which have to do with the learning of the language, the schooling of the emigrants' children in the relevant education centers, integration in the host country and coexistence with the local population, and the preservation of the Spanish language, which was also an issue of great concern for the Spanish authorities.

Another point of reiterated interest for this newspaper was to preserve an impeccable image of Spaniards living abroad. Several authors take issue with the myth of the low productivity of Spanish workers, arguing that "the Spanish emigrant working in German companies has the same productivity as Germans and much higher than that of emigrants from other nationalities" (*LR*, February 25th, 1967, 5). Moreover, "Spanish workers have increased the production thresholds in many factories," performing "in their jobs as well or even better than native workers" (*LR*, July 26th, 1967, 6). This positive stereotype that the Spanish press for the diaspora tries to disseminate is in stark contrast to that purveyed by the German press, as mentioned above, where foreign workers were associated with far less positive features.

In *Carta de España* (*CE*), a periodical publication addressed to Spanish emigrants and funded by the Spanish Ministry of Labor, we can see that this preoccupation with the image of the Spanish citizen abroad is almost a *leitmotif* throughout the main years of emigration. To quote but one example, it is quite often highlighted that Spaniards living in Germany "are exemplary even for many Germans" and that they enjoy "an excellent reputation in this country" (*CE*, March 1967, 92, 3). This image of the Spanish migrant as a hard-working, law-abiding, well-behaved person coincides with the values of the national-catholic ideology prevailing in Franco's Spain.

We could perhaps venture to suggest that the emphasis placed by this publication and others on the fact that Spaniards were as good as or even better than anybody else and that their behavior was close to ideal was perhaps an indirect revelation of the inferiority complex experienced by many emigrants, which turned at first into a feeling of melancholic absence and nostalgia for the homeland, and was later transformed into a routine that allowed for evasion to suppress their desire to return, reflected in a feeling of foreignness which was exacerbated by the ignorance of the language of the majority. This syndrome has been typified by Achotegui, a psychiatrist who works with immigrants at a Barcelona hospital, as "the Ulysses syndrome", as mentioned above (Achotegui 2009). In this vein, we may add that these emigrants spent a great deal of their free time talking to each other in their own language of their dreams of returning to places that no longer existed. They were not aware then— because of the apparently asynchronic ticking of the clocks in their two different places of reference—of the fact that their homes, their people and they themselves did not exist anymore as they previously had, which is another way of saying that they no longer lived in their idealized childhood, when they did not experience any problems of integration in the friendly environment of their natural social networks. Papastergiadis notes of this idea of asynchrony, that the Other lives in its own present but this is also the past of the host society (125). Hoerder *et al.* (2005) refer to the role of the younger generation in overcoming this time barrier:

By virtue of their age, young people are mediators between the past that serves as reference period for adults and whole societies, and the future that today's adults will experience in old age, and that today's youth will live as adults. In this continuity-providing approach, cultural negotiation and transfer is an intergenerational creative process involving choice, challenges, and changes in internally heterogeneous groups ("Introduction: Transculturation and the Accumulation of Social Capital—Understanding Histories and Decoding the Present of Young People," 12).

The younger generation may eventually change its identity or add a second identity (resulting in a hybrid, hyphenated identity), providing that the host culture is willing to accept the immigrant into the community (Weiner 1996, 53), which, obviously, is not always the case.

2.2. The Linguistic Issue in the Press

In analyzing in more detail some of the aspects that significantly affected the lives of Spanish workers who emigrated after the late Fifties, we should emphasize, as mentioned briefly above, the difficulties that they faced derived from their lack of knowledge of the host-country language(s). Unfortunately, the press does not always reflect all the facets that would interest us, particularly where the group concerned happens to lack a status that could give them a certain *power* in the social hierarchy.

Since immigrants were considered by the host society as people who would stay in the country only temporarily, they were mainly interested in them as a labor force. As for the other factors, they were considered basically as second-class citizens, who lacked a real interest in integrating themselves in the host society. This view evolved when many of the immigrants decided to renew their contracts and stay more or less permanently in the country, bringing in (if they were married) their spouses and children. In fact, children would eventually become one of the critical elements in the matter of linguistic integration.

They became essential actors in second- and third-generation contexts and on numerous occasions they were instrumental in pushing their parents—even in an unintentional manner—into learning German. (The economic value of speaking the two languages cannot be dissociated from the ethnic factor, as Pendakur / Pendakur (2002) have found in their research in the three metropolitan areas of Montreal, Toronto and Vancouver, but bilingualism adds a human capital effect which should be taken into consideration.) This at least is what we can observe in newspaper stories of the late Sixties and early Seventies, in which the Spanish emigrants themselves admit that knowing the language is no longer an insurmountable barrier but rather a tool for social progress:

> All of them can do it; German texts are easy and the patience of the teacher does the rest. It doesn't matter about the language or how old you are; as to the former, the simplicity of the texts and the interest of the teachers do the trick, and the latter is not even taken into account (*CE*, May 1972, 144, 14, translation by the authors).

In the early years of the Spanish migration, communication between the Spanish emigrants and the Germans was really a problem. Before departure, the Spanish emigrants could follow an optional four-week training module, where they were taught very basic notions of the German language. We can, thus, understand the huge difficulties they encountered at the beginning, as attested by the Spanish press reports mentioned above. Advisory service offices were established to help Spanish emigrants in the early years of the migration process to help them overcome these linguistic barriers and to offer them advice and support in different areas. These services were later integrated in different German organizations: *German Caritas, Arbeiterwohlfahrt, Diakonie*. Social workers from the countries of origin of the emigrants were in charge (*Caritas* has actually until quite recently maintained social assistance services for Italians, Portuguese, Spaniards, Croats and Poles in many German cities).

Although these social workers lacked specific training in translation or interpreting, they usually had a better knowledge of German than the newly arrived immigrants, so they often played the role of translators and interpreters. It is interesting to note that from the end of the Fifties the Spanish Institute of Emigration established many positions for pastoral advisers in Germany. These priests carried out religious (Catholic) advisory and follow-up functions with the support of the Franco regime, which wanted Spanish expatriates to keep up the religious traditions of their country while living abroad. One can see behind this policy the wish by the authorities to maintain the national-Catholic ideological orthodoxy then prevalent in Spain while at the same time guaranteeing the hard currency remittances which, together with the development of mass foreign tourism in Spain, were a key pillar of Spanish economic growth during the Sixties. The pastoral advisers, who were usually Spanish priests, often with some knowledge of German, acted as links with the network of German charitable organizations and worked hand in hand with the social workers from those organizations (A. Fernández Asperilla, in *CE*, special issue, March 2007, 38 f.).

The largest German companies did sometimes have translators, who were "sometimes other Spaniards who had arrived earlier and had learnt a little German" (Gualda Caballero 2001, 192). This was not always seen as logical by the local Spanish press. In one of the few articles devoted to the language issue we read that

> in order to be an interpreter it is necessary to have lived longer than two years in any given country as well as to have the relevant training, [...] because learning the language by ear does not qualify anyone to represent

emigrants in their dealings with the companies (*AdS*, August 4th, 1968, 8, our translation).

The author of this article goes beyond the mere description of the situation, emphasizing how important it is that German authorities get involved in this matter and ensure the quality of this service, to prevent abuses committed by the many untrained interpreters.

Besides the professional aspect of the matter, the variety of roles played by interpreters is also mentioned. Many workers saw the interpreter as the person charged with the task of "solving all the problems they may encounter in the company, defend their wishes, [...] and protect the workers when they feel they are being treated in an unfair manner by the company" (*LR*, August 25th, 1967, 5). An interpreter interviewed by *La Región* says that "la música nunca toca al gusto de todos" ["you can't please everybody"] (*LR*, August 30th, 1967, 8), and another interpreter from a German factory, Gudrun, says that many Spaniards prefer "to be taken by their hand" (*LR*, August 25th, 1967, 9). This protectionist approach was also practiced by many social mediators, whose tasks, according to their own views, went well beyond the social sphere and encompassed areas from "trying to solve, through consultation, all the social and religious problems" to linguistic mediation through "talks with employers and workers in the factories to improve working conditions" (*AdS*, July 1st, 1961, 7).

In the German press, these aspects—at first—were almost irrelevant, since they focused mainly on the other problems mentioned above. However, more recently, well after the peak period of the Spanish migration, linguistic difficulties attracted the attention not only of the German media, but also of German policymakers and legislators. Research carried out in the Nineties revealed alarming figures for school dropout and unemployment rates among foreigners, particularly those of Turkish origin (*Beauftragte der Bundesregierung für Migration, Flüchtlinge und Integration*, 2010). Fluency in German seemed to be logically linked to an optimal use of all the educational and professional opportunities, as well as to a much more effective integration in the labor market.

Although we cannot delve here into the political and historical factors that contributed to a change of direction in German policies (and politics), it is clear that in 2005 the debate about the integration of foreigners in Germany—these making up a total of 6.7 million in that year—led to the enactment of the new Foreigners Act, which among other things compels foreign citizens to prove a sufficient knowledge of German if they wish to legalize their situation, obtain a residence permit or acquire German nationality (the relevant paragraphs of the *Ausländergesetz* of January 1st, 2005, being "§ 9 Abs. 2 Satz 1 Nr. 7 i. V. m. § 9 Abs. 2 Satz 2 des § 10, Abs. 3 i. V. m. § 11 Satz 1 Nr. 1").

The statement, repeated *ad nauseam*, "Deutschland ist kein Einwanderungsland" ("Germany is not a country of immigration") (see *Die Zeit*, April 12th, 2006) led finally to the *Integrationspolitik*. This policy is aimed at integrating Germany's foreign citizens through the implementation of different measures, among which we should note regulations on subsidized integration courses—or, more precisely, German language and culture courses—, which, despite their voluntary nature, are in the long run prescriptive and a necessary prerequisite for applications for certain social benefits, employment, *etc.* These measures are being implemented with the support of the German Federal Government and the *Länder* (state) administrations, which are contributing considerable sums of money to the relevant organizations in charge of the program. The impact of the measures, however, remains to be seen, taking into account the brief period that they have been in place. But research carried out in the Netherlands, where similar legislation was enacted in 1998 (*Wet Inburgering Nieuwkomers*), concluded that "neither knowledge of the Dutch language, nor obtaining a higher degree in the Netherlands, is enough for integration in the Dutch labour force" (Ghorashi / van Tilburg 2006,

62). So language acquisition seems to be only one part of the integration process (Weiner, 52 f.).

3. Discussion

WE HAVE SEEN examples of how the language barrier issue was perceived by public opinion, by immigrants and by the authorities in the United States and in Germany in two different periods of our modern history. Some of these points invite further discussion.

We believe that the press, in the past and in the present, has tended to overlook the communication difficulties experienced by people who do not understand each other, perpetuating a fictional image according to which conversations among people from different languages and cultures simply *happen*, and we read works and we watch films as if they had been written or shot in our own languages. We are aware of the great influence of the media in shaping public opinion—as the philosopher Epictetus (55 AD) once said, "Men are disturbed not by things, but by the view which they take of them"—, and perhaps that is why it is worth emphasizing that, behind an apparently smooth universal intercommunication paradise, a totally different reality hides, in which millions of daily bilingual exchanges and translated words take place at all levels in our societies. The limits to the *curse of Babel* are set precisely by the countless interpreters, from the anonymous and spontaneous *ad hoc* passer-by to the well-known professional, and translators. That is why these linguistic mediators cannot possibly fit into one unique definition of interpreter or translator.

Sometimes the media seem to be suddenly aware of the multilingual reality that surrounds us and they make it a news story by calling attention to the feats of a polyglot child or the troubles experienced in looking for an appropriate mediator for certain settings. The opinions expressed by the press can be only one of the many pieces of the puzzle in which social phenomena are represented and, in that context, the articles which appear in newspapers or magazines are, when read critically between the lines, an important source of information for grasping the social perception of mediated situations. But, as research in the field of migration in modern societies has shown, the topic of language mediation is only one side of a much more complex social issue, which requires a multidisciplinary approach.

Migration patterns have changed with the passing of time and the revolutions in transport and communications. They are no longer characterized by the old no-return journey over-seas, but rather by relatively easy regular travel between the two places. For instance, European emigrants to the United States around 1900 left their country with little expectation of going back there anytime soon, so that they (and their children) needed to adapt to the host country as soon as possible. Latin American or Asian immigrants in the United States today are usually able to travel quite often to their countries of origin and to keep close ties with the family and society in their place of origin via satellite communication—you can watch your local TV station almost anywhere now——and the Internet.

This is also what happens with expatriates from Northern European countries in sunny coastal parts of Spain. Retirement migration has turned certain seaside resorts in Spain into a real geriatric coast, where, according to Betty / Cahill (2000), "The vast majority of British residents read only British newspapers, listen to English speaking community radio stations, and watch satellite television" (97). Or, as O'Reilly (2000) says: "I met people who had lived in the area 30 years and who spoke fewer than 20 words of Spanish. In fact it is possible to get by quite well without learning Spanish" (240).

The concept of *home* has now acquired many qualifications and nuances which pertain to the sense of place and sense of belonging, to the building of imaginary spaces both in the place of origin and in the place of destination (see Salih 2001). Indeed:

> Research with regard to Turks in Germany has re-
> vealed a notable finding; namely that the interviewees

feel a sense of belonging primarily to their German place of residence, despite thoroughly rejecting any identification for themselves with "the Germans" (Sackmann 2003, 237).

If Spanish emigrants in the Sixties—often unable to return to their homes back in Spain for a number of years—suffered from the "Ulysses syndrome", it seems that the recent information and telecommunication technologies might be an antidote against that. This ubiquitous umbilical cord with one's language and culture entails, however, other risks, such as the clustering in almost self-sufficient neighborhoods, a lesser need for integration into the host society—where they feel they are staying only temporarily—and, therefore, a greater need for social, cultural and linguistic mediators when the migrants have to deal with the majority group. The pro minority human rights movement has also played a role in encouraging respect for the linguistic and cultural rights of immigrants, making our modern societies more multicultural but not necessarily more intercultural, and indeed moving them even farther from the "melting pot" situation. Perhaps this is why the demand for translation and interpreting services in the United States has continued to rise.

It would seem that the main cause of the lack of integration of immigrants in host societies is not so much the linguistic or cultural divide but the prevalence of negative images of migrants. These images, conveyed by the media, and policies which aim at highlighting differences rather than commonalities—such as the *us vs. them* stereotype that tends to show nationals as victims of the foreigners—may lead to apocalyptic predictions of disintegration of the nation. A recent example is Thilo Sarrazin's controversial book *Deutschland schafft sich ab* ("Germany does away with itself", 2010), in which, among other things, he blames Muslims in Germany for their unwillingness to integrate and for their abuse of the German social services, and predicts that Muslims will soon overwhelm the German population due to their high birth rates.

Historical research suggests that the endeavor of changing mentalities—and the concept of *culture* has a lot to do with worldviews and traditions—requires periods of time, sometimes longer than a generation, to succeed. Our societies are characterized by a mosaic of linguistic groups, with harmonious notes at community level but with an apparent cacophony at the metropolitan, regional or national level.

The effort made by German authorities in recent legislation to push prospective immigrants to learn the language of the country seems to point to a certain (perceived) correlation between command of the language and social integration, but it remains to be seen 1) whether or not this is a sufficient incentive for immigrants to learn the language, and 2) whether or not a good command of the host country's language will be enough to secure integration. The fact that third-generation descendants of Turkish immigrants in Germany who are fluent in German are still far from being perceived by many groups as fully fledged Germans seems to contradict the apparent logic of the legal provisions. Perhaps we should reflect on the fact that we are applying a nation-state paradigm here when what we are actually facing are postnational formations (Nuhoglu Soysal 1994, 167), in which there can be many paths to integration, depending on *the type and extent of the assimilation involved* (Sackmann, 238).

References

Achotegui Lozate, Joseba. *Emigrar en el siglo XXI: El síndrome del inmigrante con estrés crónico y múltiple-síndrome de Ulises*. Llançà: Ediciones El mundo de la mente, 2009.

Alonso, Icíar / Baigorri, Jesús / Payàs, Gertrudis. "Nahuatlatos y familias de intérpretes en el México colonial." In: *1611: Revista de Historia de la Traducción*, 2, 2008. Website, <http://www. traduccionliteraria.org/1611/art/alonso-baigorri-payas. htm>

------------- / Payàs, Gertrudis. "Sobre alfaqueques y nahuatlatos: Nuevas aportaciones a la historia de la interpretación." In:

Investigación y práctica en traducción e interpretación en los servicios públicos: Desafíos y alianzas. Ed. C. Valero-Garcés. CD-ROM. Alcalá de Henares: Universidad de Alcalá, 2008, 39-52.

Anthias, Floya / Lazaridis, Gabriella (Eds.). *Gender and Migration in Southern Europe: Women on the Move.* Oxford: Berg, 2000.

Baigorri, Jesús / Alonso, Icíar. "Lenguas indígenas y mediación lingüística en las reducciones jesuíticas del Paraguay (s. XVII)." In: *Mediazioni online: Revista online di studi interdisciplinari su lingue e culture.* Bologna: Università degli Studi di Bologna e Gedit Edizioni, December 2007. Website, <http://www.mediazionionline.it/articoli/baigorri-alonso.html>

Beauftragte der Bundesregierung für Migration, Flüchtlinge und Integration, Die. *8. Bericht der Bundesregierung über die Lage der Ausländerinnen und Ausländer in Deutschland.* June 2010. Website, <http://www.bundesregierung.de/Content/DE/__Anlagen/2010/2010-07-07-langfassung-lagebericht-ib,property=publicationFile.pdf>

Betty, Charles / Cahill, Michael. "British Expatriates' Experience of Health and Social Services on the Costa del Sol" (2000). In: *Gender and Migration in Southern Europe.* Ed. F. Anthias / G. Lazaridis, 83-103.

Carnevale, Nancy C. *A New Language, a New World: Italian Immigrants in the United States, 1890-1945.* Urbana & Chicago, IL: University of Illinois Press, 2009.

Díaz del Castillo, Bernal. *Historia verdadera de la conquista de la Nueva España* (1632). Madrid: Editorial Dastin, 1982.

Ghorashi, Halleh / van Tilburg, Maria. "'When is my Dutch Good Enough?': Experiences of Refugee Women with Dutch Labour Organizations." In: *Journal of International Migration and Integration*, 7, 1, 2006, 51-70.

Golash-Boza, T. "Assessing the Advantages of Bilingualism for the Children of Immigrants." In: *International Migration Review*, 39, 3, Fall 2005, 721-53.

Grupo Alfaqueque. *Los límites de Babel: Ensayos sobre la*

comunicación entre lenguas y culturas. Madrid / Frankfurt/M.: Editorial Iberoamericana / Vervuert, 2010.

Gualda Caballero, E. "El trabajo social en Alemania con los *Gastarbeiter* o emigrantes económicos españoles." In: *Portularia 1* (Universidad de Huelva), 2001, 185-202.

Hoerder, Dirk. "The Global and the Local in Migrants' Experiences: Multiple Social Spaces in a Long-term Perspective." In: Hoerder *et al.* (Eds.), 235-51.

------------ / Hébert, Yvonne / Schmitt, Irina (Eds.). *Negotiating Transcultural Lives: Belongings and Social Capital among Youth in Comparative Perspective.* Göttingen: V & R Unipress, 2005.

Igartua, Juan José / Muñiz, Carlos (Eds.). *Medios de Comunicación, Inmigración y Sociedad.* Salamanca: Ediciones Universidad de Salamanca, 2007.

Karttunen, Frances. *Between Worlds: Interpreters, Guides and Survivors.* New Brunswick, NJ: Rutgers University Press, 1994.

King, Russell / Wood, Nancy (Eds.). *Media and Migration: Constructions of Mobility and Difference.* London: Routledge, 2001.

Limage, L. J. "Policy Aspects of Educational Provision for Children of Migrants in Western European Schools." In: *International Migration*, XXIII, 2, June 1985, 251-62.

MacFarlane, Karen. "Understanding Justice: Criminal Courtroom Interpretation in Eighteenth-Century London and Twenty-First-Century Toronto." In: *TTR (traduction, terminologie, redaction)*, XX, 2, 2007, 271-99.

Nuhoglu Soysal, Yasemin. *Limits of Citizenship: Migrants and Postnational Membership in Europe.* Chicago: The University of Chicago Press, 1994.

O'Reilly, Karen. "Trading Intimacy for Liberty: British Women on the Costa del Sol" (2000). In: *Gender and Migration in Southern Europe.* Ed. F. Anthias / G. Lazaridis, 227-48.

------------ . "Blackpool in the Sun: Images of the British on the Costa del Sol" (2001). In: *Media and Migration.* Ed. R. King

/ N. Wood, 173-88.

Papastergiadis, Nikos. *The Turbulence of Migration: Globalization, Deterritorialization and Hybridity.* Cambridge: Polity Press, 1999.

Pendakur, Krishna / Pendakur, Ravi. "Language as Both Human Capital and Ethnicity." In: *International Migration Review*, 36, 1, Spring 2002, 147-77.

Penninx, Rinus / Kraal, Karen / Martiniello, Marco / Vertovec, Steven (Eds.). *Citizenship in European Cities: Immigrants, Local Politics and Integration Policies*, Aldershot, Hants.: Ashgate, 2004.

Prieto Ramos, Fernando. *Media & Migrants: A Critical Analysis of Spanish and Irish Discourses on Immigration.* Frankfurt/M.: Peter Lang, 2004.

Sackmann, Rosemarie. "Postscript: Cultural Difference and Collective Identity in Processes of Integration." In: *Identity and Integration: Migrants in Western Europe.* Ed. Rosemarie Sackmann / Bernhard Peters / Thomas Faist. Aldershot, Hants.: Ashgate, 2003, 235-43.

Salih, Ruba. "Shifting Meanings of 'Home': Consumption and Identity in Moroccan Women's Transnational Practices between Italy and Morocco." In: *New Approaches to Migration?: Transnational Communities and the Transformation of Home.* Ed. Nadje Al-Ali / Khalid Koser. London: Routledge, 2001, 51-67.

Sarrazin, Thilo. *Deutschland schafft sich ab: Wie wir unser Land aufs Spiel setzen.* Munich: DVA, 2010.

Todorov, Tzvetan. *The Fear of Barbarians: Beyond the Clash of Civilizations* [*La Peur des barbares: Au-delà du choc des civilisations*, 2008]. Transl. Andrew Brown. Cambridge: Polity Press, 2010.

Van Dijk, Teun A. *Ideología y discurso.* Barcelona: Ariel, 2003.

Weiner, Myron. "Determinants of Immigrant Integration: An International Comparative Analysis." In: *Immigration and Integration in Post-Industrial Societies: Theoretical Analysis and Policy-Related Research.* Ed. Naomi Carmon. London: Macmillan, 1996, 46-64.

NOTE: For convenience, the issues and dates for press sources such as *El Adelanto de Salamanca,* the *Boston Daily Globe, Carta de España, Der Spiegel, La Región, Newsweek,* the *New York Times,* the *Toronto Star* and *Die Zeit* are given in the text.

The **Alfaqueque Research Group** (www.usal.es/~alfaqueque/) has the following members (with their respective universities): Jesús Baigorri Jalón (dir.) (Salamanca), Icíar Alonso Araguás (Salamanca), Concepción Otero Moreno (Hildesheim), Gertrudis Payàs Puigarnau (Católica, Temuco), Mariachiara Russo (Bologna-Forlì) and Críspulo Travieso Rodríguez (Salamanca).

This research received financial support from project HUM2006-0543/FILO of the Spanish Ministry of Education and Science.

PUT THE SIGNS UP, TAKE THE SIGNS DOWN
SOME QUESTIONS OF LANGUAGE, POLITICS, AND IDENTITY
by FRANCIS JARMAN

MANY WESTERN EUROPEAN countries have large ethnic minority groups originating from outside Europe and outside Western culture. They came when they were needed economically; in some cases (Britain and France) they were encouraged to come by ties created during the colonial period; and, in the light of the demographic catastrophe now confronting much of Western Europe, it is probably good that they are here. However, for the mainstream cultures and their new minorities, learning to live together has not been an easy ride, marked as it has been (at different stages) by social and workplace discrimination, "race riots", ghettoization, tensions between minorities and the police, extremist backlash, calls for repatriation, support from members of minority groups for international terrorism, and excessive preoccupation with the special "rights" and "needs" of minorities. It is this last point which prompted the writing of this short essay.

A few years ago I took part in a weekend conference organized by the Turkish Federation of a large German city in cooperation with that city's Job Centres (*Arbeitsämter*). Its purpose was to encourage better intercultural communication between young members of minority groups and the German civil servants working to help them, against a background of previous and continuing tensions. One sensitive point had been the debate about whether to remove signs in Turkish from certain government buildings. There were good arguments for taking them down: the unemployed Turkish youngsters were normally fluent in German anyway, and the signs could be taken as discrimination against members of other minority groups, such as young Russians, for whom no signs had been provided. On the other hand, if the signs remained they would be appreciated by the older generation of Turkish Germans, some of whom had only a restricted command of German, and they would signal a respect for their culture and a willingness on the part of the authorities to take their problems seriously.

Nobody at the conference was so ill-mannered as to ask, "Why can't they learn German? After all, they're living in Germany, aren't they?" This has been one of the uglier sights and sounds of postwar German life—the bullying of some unfortunate and incoherent alien by an officious bus driver, station master or some other person (often in uniform) with the exhortation: "Speak German! This here is Germany!" I have witnessed scenes like this several times, and I am not for one moment advocating this kind of rudeness. However, the question (when raised more tactfully) is a fair one. Integration into the broader community is not likely to happen for people who are unable or unwilling to learn the language. It need not, moreover, amount to total assimilation, meaning that the immigrants' culture effectively disappears within a couple of generations, except perhaps for such traces as an exotic-sounding name; in successful integration, the immigrants retain some at least of their cultural and linguistic heritage, in the way that "hyphenated Americans"—Irish-Americans, Italian-Americans, Japanese-Americans, etc.—have managed to do, while internalizing core values of the host culture.

Arguing for integration with any degree of robustness goes against the grain of multiculturalism, the dominant cultural ideology among Western European liberals until quite recent times. The multiculturalist mindset is relativist, requiring that the cultural behavior patterns of ethnic minorities be respected *per se*. Minority group members can best fulfil themselves if they are allowed to follow their authentic traditions, even if these happen to be at odds with those of the indigenous culture. The wider community will only gain from this, because out of cultural diversity exciting synergies can be created. (This is undoubtedly true, but it requires dialog, not stand-off confrontation.) There is also a tendency to regard non-Western ways as being in any case inherently superior, because closer to nature, less materialistic, and less selfishly individualistic. So much for the theory, which achieved an almost knee-jerk level of acceptance among members of the educated classes in Western Europe, including many who would feel uncomfortable if Asian or African families actually moved in as their neighbors.

While it was certainly a good thing, after centuries of colonial exploitation and cultural chauvinism, for the West to adopt a less contemptuous attitude towards the Rest, the pendulum swung out rather too far. In its willingness to sentimentalize the non-Western Other, and to suspend criticism of cultural attitudes or forms of behavior that by modern Western standards seem backward, oppressive or just downright disgusting (Jarman, *Burning Women*), relativistic multiculturalism is hardly healthier as a moral and intellectual position than old-fashioned racism. It is not only masochistic (an understandable hangover of guilt from colonialism) but also self-deluding, in the sense that it is a characteristically Western stance, not widely shared by people in the non-Western world, many of whom for their part are less than willing to be "tolerant" or "respectful" of what they see as degenerate Western ways.

There is now a perceptible withdrawal from multiculturalism going on in much of Europe. In a widely quoted survey of the main intellectual events of 2006, the social commentator Bryan Appleyard pronounced that the demise of multiculturalism had been one of the "big ideas" of the year:

Multiculturalism is dead. It had it coming. An ideology that defined a nation as a series of discrete cultural and political entities that were each free to opt out of any or all common orthodoxies was never a serious contender in the Miss Best Political System pageant.

[Since this essay was first drafted, for inclusion in a *Festschrift* in 2008, there have been a number of highly publicized declarations by political leaders on the failure of multiculturalism, including speeches by the former Australian premier John Howard in September 2010, German chancellor Angela Merkel in October 2010 and British prime minister David Cameron and French president Nicolas Sarkozy in February 2011; former Spanish premier José María Aznar had already branded multiculturalism "a big failure" in a speech at Georgetown University in October 2006.]

Unfortunately, the cultural damage has already been done. As a consequence of multiculturalism, parallel societies were allowed to form in many Western European countries. In the Netherlands, this development fitted neatly into the pattern of an existing social phenomenon known as *pillarization*, in which groups with different political or religious identities organized their own parallel social and cultural infrastructures. In Britain, it happened more by *laissez-faire* default, although encouraged by policies of keeping a relatively open door to extremist and radical groups, provided that they projected their more vicious activities outside the United Kingdom—an attitude, much criticized by Britain's neighbors, that became known as *Londonistan* (Phillips 2006) and has gone badly wrong since 9/11. The existence of parallel societies allowed non- and sometimes anti-Western values and attitudes to flourish. For example, a survey among British Muslims (GfK 2006) showed 34 per cent of the 18-24 year-olds expressing a wish to live under Sharia law, 51 per cent of the same age-group believing that 9/11 was a conspiracy by the United States and Israel, and 31 per cent claiming that the July 2005 bomb attacks in London were justified. Less spectacularly, though with the potential to create immense social conflict in the long term, parallel societies cushion their members against pressure to integrate or to adopt the values of the broader community.

This functions in different ways, although with language as the common denominator. On the simple level of *communication*, lack of knowledge of the host culture's language will mean less interaction, less mutual understanding, and less likelihood of a common cultural identity being achieved—in other words, no integration. Let us take Sweden as an example. In Sweden, the "foreign-born", many of whom are Muslim, make up about twelve per cent of the population (and those with a culturally "foreign" background double that figure). According to the Minister for Integration and Equality, Nyamko Sabuni, herself a Muslim of African origin, the country has been only moderately successful in integrating its non-Western immigrants. It would help greatly, she declared, if all of them would try to become proficient in Swedish:

> Language and jobs are the two most crucial things for integration. If you want to become a Swedish citizen, we think you should have some basic knowledge of Swedish. [...] We have a whole underclass of people who don't have jobs, who don't speak the language and who are living on the fringes of society (quoted in Powell 2006).

One reason for the success of the United States as a country of immigration was the socialization of successive immigrant groups into America's "Anglo-Protestant" mainstream culture by means of the English language. In his study of American national identity, Samuel P. Huntington (2004) quotes with approval Unamuno's dictum that "Language is the blood of the spirit" and describes it as "the basis of community" (159). When people share a language they can speak to each other and read what the other writes. Without a shared language, parallel cultures and separate arenas of communication will develop, and a society or nation will polarize. Huntington warns explicitly of this happening in the modern-day United States as a result of the demands being made by Mexican-Americans and other Hispanics for equal status for their language, Spanish, especially in schools.

> Bilingual education has been a euphemism for teaching students in Spanish and immersing them in Hispanic culture. The children of past generations of immigrants did not have such programs, became fluent in English, and absorbed America's culture. The children of contemporary non-Hispanic immigrants by and large learn English and assimilate into American society faster than those of Hispanic immigrants (320 f.).

For those who are frightened of losing their cultural *identity* as a consequence of being in an alien cultural environment, it is essential to maintain a psychological cocoon against what is threateningly strange by staying in the reassuring ambience of their own language. No one has expressed this better than the Turkish novelist Orhan Pamuk. In *Snow* (2002), the writer Ka, living in exile in Germany, firmly resists learning German: "'Was it hard for you in Germany?' asked Ipek. 'The thing that saved me was not learning German,' said Ka. 'My body rejected the language, and that was how I was able to preserve my purity and my soul'" (33). He travels across Germany, giving poetry readings to Turkish immigrants. Although he observes German life, it is "through the smoky glass of the [train] window" (*ibid.*)—a metaphor of cultural distance, of being within a safe "culture bubble", used by many writers, including J. G. Ballard in *Empire of the Sun* (1984, see also Jarman, *Ballard*, 63)—and: "Because he could not understand the language, he felt as safe, as comfortable, as if he were sitting in his own house, and this was when he wrote his poems" (Pamuk, 33).

The reassurance comes about because in your own language words mean what you think you know they mean, and aren't the weaselly things that they can become in translation. For example, a Pakistani's *Izzat* is not the same as an Englishman's "honor", and the English term "honor killing" is not an adequate description of what it refers to from *either* point of view. German *Faulheit* has a moral dimension by association that is not present in English "laziness"—because *faul* can mean "rotten", as well as "lazy". And so on. For members of a minority culture, not knowing the language of the host culture can be a safeguard against exposure to its corrosive *values*. In most cases it is primarily the women and girls who must be "protected", ostensibly against immorality. In effect, though, this enforced linguistic purdah, like the actual physical variety, is to prevent them taking control of their own lives and deciding for themselves matters of education, work, sexuality and marriage. The Bangladeshi human rights lawyer Zia Haider Rahman (2006) has described the situation in Tower Hamlets in the East End of London (an area, like Bradford in Yorkshire, where there are a significant number of ethnic minority women who are prevented from learning English):

> Perverse values that are anathema to liberal ideals fester behind the language barrier in the East End. Many men in the Bangladeshi community forbid women from learning English for the same reason that they won't let their women venture out. I was shaken recently to hear a Bangladeshi woman who had lived here for 22 years say that her golden years had been wasted. If only she had learnt English, she said, she could have spoken to people and discovered other lives. She said women were not allowed out for fear of being corrupted, of gaining courage or running away. If they learnt English they might rise above their station.

With heavy but justifiable sarcasm, Rahman makes the point that multiculturalists fail to call attention to these abuses "presumably because they are busy arranging diversity training for the rest of us". Perhaps the greatest tragedy of Western European multiculturalism has been its collusion, while all the time paying lip service to a progressive ideal, with the forces of oppression, male chauvinism and cruelty in non-Western societies and its betrayal of the modernizers, the secularists—and the feminists.

> In its demand for equality for women, feminism sets itself in opposition to virtually every culture on earth. You could say that multiculturalism demands respect for all cultural traditions, while feminism interrogates and challenges all cultural traditions. [...F]undamentally, the ethical claims of feminism run counter to the cultural relativism of [...] multiculturalism (Pollitt 1999, 27, see also Jarman, *Burning Women*).

It is minority women and girls who have paid the highest price for our fastidious relativism. Enabling and encouraging them to learn the language of the country that they are living in would constitute major progress towards long-term integration, but they are often under pressure from within their own communities not to take such a step.

In Britain, they are further discouraged by the zealous willingness of local authorities and public services to help them by translating everything into any language. In 2006 BBC researchers uncovered annual public expenditure figures for translation services of more than £100 million: local councils had spent at least £25 million, the police £21 million, the courts more than £10 million (without including costs incurred in connection with legal aid) and the National Health Service £55 million at the very least. Some individual London hospitals were spending £1 million each on translation services, Mostly to pay for interpreters for consultations between doctors and non-English-speaking patients. The town of Peterborough (with a population of about 150,000) had also spent more than £1 million on translation and interpreting services involving 76 separate languages, Peterborough council seeing it as its duty "to translate into any dialect or language for which there is a demand" (figures and quotation from Easton 2006).

To write in a *Festschrift* honoring an eminent specialist in linguistics and translation [see the note at the end of this essay] that there can, under certain circumstances, sometimes be *too much* of the latter may seem like *lèse majesté*, but Reiner Arntz is also a distinguished scholar in the field of language and politics. Telling members of ethnic minorities that we should like them to integrate, please—and learn our language, naturally—while at the same time blanketing them with translations and interpreting services is no less than a classic double bind. As Rahman's Bangladeshi friend from Tower Hamlets explained to the BBC,

> however well-meaning, all the language support had ruined her life. "When you are trying to help us, you are actually harming us. [...] All we have to do is say hello and they are here with their interpreters. We just sit here doing nothing and we don't need to speak in English at all" (Easton).

There should by all means be help and practical support, especially when this takes the form of language classes and social and cultural activities. A mentoring scheme which "twinned" members of a minority group with members of the broader community (though with ordinary people, not interpreters or social workers) would also be a good idea, socially, politically, and linguistically, despite the resistance it would encounter from the traditionalists. There are many different things that can be done to foster harmony and integration—but I am strongly in favor of taking down the signs.

References

Appleyard, Bryan. "Eureka." In: *The Sunday Times*, December 17th, 2006. Website, <www.timesonline.co.uk/tol/news/article755989.ece>

Ballard, J. G. *Empire of the Sun*. London: Gollancz, 1984.

Easton, Mark. "Cost in Translation." In: *BBC News*, December 12th, 2006. Website, <http://news.bbc.co.uk/2/hi/uk_news/6172805.stm>

GfK (Growth from Knowledge) NOP Social Research (2006). "Attitudes to Living in Britain—A Survey of Muslim Opinion. For Channel 4 *Dispatches*." Website, accessed last on 5.02.2010, <www.imaginate.uk.com/MCC01_SURVEY/Site%20Download.pdf>

Huntington, Samuel P. *Who Are We?—The Challenges to America's National Identity*. New York: Simon & Schuster, 2004.

Jarman, Francis. "J. G. Ballard: Through the Eyes of a Child." In: Francis Jarman. *White Skin, Dark Skin, Power, Dream: Collected Essays on Literature and Culture*. Holicong, PA: Borgo/Wildside, 2005, 57-68.

------------. "*Burning Women*." In: Francis Jarman. *White Skin, Dark Skin, Power, Dream*, 95-121.

Pamuk, Orhan. *Snow* [*Kar*, 2002]. Transl. M. Freely. London: Faber, 2004.

Phillips, Melanie. *Londonistan—How Britain Is Creating a Terror State Within*. London: Gibson Square, 2006.

Pollitt, Katha. "Whose Culture?" In: *Is Multiculturalism Bad for Women?* Ed. Susan Moller Okin *et al.* Princeton, NJ: Princeton University Press, 1999, 27-30.

Powell, Helena Frith. "Sweden's Muslim Minister Turns on Veil." In: *The Sunday Times*, October 22nd, 2006, I 23.

Rahman, Zia Haider. "Hope of Escape Lost in Translation." In: *The Sunday Times*, December 17th, 2006, IV 2.

NOTE: Only a few very small changes and corrections have

been made to the text, which was originally a contribution to a *Festschrift* in honor of the German linguist Reiner Arntz:

Krings, H.-P. / Mayer, F. (Eds.). *Sprachenvielfalt im Kontext von Fachkommunikation, Übersetzung und Fremdsprachenunterricht: Für Reiner Arntz zum 65. Geburtstag.* Berlin: Frank & Timme, 2008.

The essay is republished here by kind permission of the publishers, Frank & Timme GmbH, Verlag für wissenschaftliche Literatur, Berlin.

IN QUEST OF THE LANGUAGE BRIDGE

by Ekaterina Sofronieva

THERE IS A click and my computer goes off. I stare at the empty screen and savor the silence. I reach out for my pen and find myself fidgeting with it for far too long. How do I grade the performance of a good teacher in a poor foreign language classroom?

I played the video in my mind over and over again. In an "open lesson" when parents, teachers and the school principal are present, children show their mastery of English as a foreign language. The lesson is fast-paced, my teacher trainee engages the children in all sorts of games, pair work, team work, all done by the book. Yet, there is something wrong in the picture. It might just as well have been a quiz lesson in geography or history, in which pupils denote things, name the capital cities of countries, repeat dates and events. And right answers count. Anything that requires explicit memory. But not language. Language is not about naming objects, reciting poems or producing words on demand. I was tempted to count the actual minutes of "English" that there had been in those forty minutes of the lesson, but dismissed the thought. A great deal had been in Bulgarian—instructions, grouping and regrouping, the organizing games and activities, the giving of feedback, comments and praise. What is the value of a game in English that is played in three minutes if it takes ten minutes to explain beforehand in the learners' mother tongue? The children peer into their English books to read, but are then required to hum *in Bulgarian*. That dumbfounded me. Mothers and teachers are beaming at what apparently has been felt by all to be the completion of another successful exercise in testing children's comprehension skills. Are these our future European interpreters and translators?

At the end of the lesson children are engaged in "dialogism". Two volunteers run to the board, in front of the class, to make use of their language skills in a dialog, encouraged to create "a real life communicative exchange". The concept of dialogism, extensively researched by Seppo Tella and Marja Mononen-Aaltonen at the Media Centre of the University of Helsinki (1998), has been defined by them as follows:

> Dialogue is a crucial element in the creation of any language organization and especially in the establishing collaboration and network environment. It suggests that the learning environment in the framework of dialogism cannot be a physical space, a classroom, not any particular media educational tool. The learning environment is—dialogue (103).

"What's your name?" the little girl asks automatically, in a chase for an answer that they all know anyway. After all the activities, the effort and time spent on the language, this is the question that inevitably comes to mind first. It lacks emotion, the feeling of anticipation that is needed for real communication to take place, and any reason why it should be posed at all between school mates who know each other's names. I switch off the computer, but a bitter aftertaste is still there.

BULGARIA IS NO different from other European countries. There are plenty of bright children and many wonderful teachers. However, my video is far from unique as a record of language performance in a traditional foreign language classroom with smart children and a popular teacher. A lot has been written and said in the twenty-first century about early foreign language acquisition and the need for change in education, exploiting children's natural capacity to acquire languages, and supporting the development and expression of their potential as they interact in a new cultural-social environment. However, traditional methodologies have clearly failed to equip language teachers with the strategies needed for full development of children's foreign language skills and simultaneous enhancement of their physical, emotional and psychological growth in a new language environment. There are many techniques on offer that can be applied and integrated into language classes, but in most instances there is lack of a consistent and holistic language methodological framework to bind all of them together. The new requirements made of the language teachers are well understood, yet somehow many teachers are still left on their own in the classroom to rely mainly on their own resources, creativity and personality. It may be easy in words, but apparently it is difficult and insufficient in reality.

> Traditionally, the style of training offered to language teachers in Italy (and in other European countries) has always been rather academic, providing a sweeping and generic lump of theoretical knowledge and abandoning teachers to do the job of translating what they've learnt into real classroom activities and teaching materials. Though this sort of training may be culturally enriching, experience has shown that it contributes little to teachers' professional skills. Having completed the training course teachers too often find themselves at a loss as to how to apply what they have learnt and end up turning back to the usual text books (Taeschner 2005, 5).

In the United States, Linda Zientek (2007) has written on teacher preparedness in connection with the growth of alternative teacher certification programs in the Nineties. In her view, our main concern should not be with whether or not these programs should exist, but with whether teacher preparation programs are effective and produce high quality teachers (960). One fair point that she makes with respect to the growing demands and expectations of society *vis-à-vis* its teachers is that we should be looking initially into whether the teachers have been provided with the necessary methodology and teaching strategies for the classroom.

> In the pursuit of preparing teachers who can teach all students, the educational community needs to determine if teachers are being armed with the necessary skills to feel prepared in the classroom and what factors best contribute to teachers' perceptions of preparedness (998).

In spite of the existing attempts to shape and apply innovative, better strategies, and offer different programs to teachers, the gap between theory and practice is still strongly felt in many foreign language classrooms. The video came as a cold illustration and a reminder. As an educator, university lecturer and teacher trainer I felt a debt to teachers and children.

TWO MONTHS LATER I met Professor Traute Taeschner in Rome and my life changed. A mother of two, a professor of psychology, of German origin, born in Brazil but living and working in Italy, with a command of five languages, this refined lady had all the answers I needed. In a week's training, she built the beautiful rock-solid bridge between theory and practice that I had been in quest of.

TWO YEARS LATER I stand behind the camera in the nursery yard.

We had arrived late on a hot summer day, right after the children had been taken out to play. Just as my team of students and I were exchanging glances and deciding what to do, a kid turned around and saw us. She screamed to everyone at the top of her voice "They are here, they are here" and in a flash the group was rushing towards us.

Click. My second-year university students of preschool education help the children to put on their white T-shirts with the lovable orange images of Hocus and Lotus, the two little dinocrocs, printed on them. A torrent of hugs and kisses follows. Then the students slip away, leaving the one who is to lead the lesson among thirty thrilled children. They hold their hands out to form a big circle. I hear my trainee's voice calming their chirrup of excitement:

"Now, let's hold hands, close your eyes, one, two, three, four, five..."

They count to ten, soon to be "transported" into a magic world of adventure and play. A sudden exclamation in Bulgarian unexpectedly merges into the video sound: "Oh, they are coming back!" It originates from behind me, where the kids' nursery teacher is standing to watch. She comes forward and swiftly helps two boys, who because of their parents' early arrival had been dragged away from the group just before the circle was formed, to get back into their Hocus and Lotus T-shirts. The boys triumphantly rejoin the circle. The parents withdraw to the fence and watch the spectacle from a distance.

"Once upon a time...there was a little Dinocroc.... His name was Hocus...and...he wanted to play."

My young trainee and the children, eyes wide open now, have started the adventure. She speaks enigmatically and smiles at the children, giving them time to repeat and savor the experience. Her verbal behavior is supported by actions and gestures. She steps out of the circle and back in again to distinguish the roles of the narrator and the story characters.

"I'm a little Dinocroc,...I'm walking in the park... Who wants to play a game with me...? Who wants to play?"

The string of events is acted out and voiced in smaller parts by the walking and talking dinocrocs. Eyebrows raised, hands spread in anticipation of a friend to play with.

"A tiny yellow butterfly...was flying near Hocus.... The

butterfly said ..."

Thirty "little butterflies" of entwined hands are flying about in the air. I spot a peculiar red one that stands out— it belongs to a boy who is still wearing his football gloves, from a game that he deserted to join the circle. Boys and girls are mirroring my teacher trainee in every movement that she makes, every raising of voice or eyebrow, words uttered and gestures made. Curious parents, standing by the fence, are left unnoticed.

At the end of the lesson the parents besiege me. "What did you do to make all those children, thirty of them, stay involved, speaking English only for all that time?" I smile back. "I didn't do anything. My student did."

The truth is that unless you join the circle and take part with the children, you may never find out. For you need to experience it, experience the power and beauty of bonding and communication in this new language environment.

The children don't want to take their T-shirts off. Some have already headed for the classroom. They want to sing and dance to the mini-musical, look through the Dino books and watch the cartoon, activities that follow the acting. My army of students, scattered around, regroups once again to accomplish these tasks. The parents may have to wait a little bit longer...

THE NARRATIVE FORMAT *The Adventures of Hocus and Lotus* is an innovative, psycholinguistic approach to teaching and learning languages created by Professor Taeschner, who works in the Faculty of Psychology at the University of Rome ("La Sapienza"). Her extensive research and findings in the field of early foreign language acquisition led to the creation of this model in the Nineties. Its further development, diffusion and implementation have been financed in a series of European projects. Many partners, collaborators and specialists of different nationalities in the fields of psychology, linguistics, mass media and education have contributed to the team's efforts. It has won numerous awards, among them the prize for Best Soundtrack at the Dervio International Cartoon Festival, 2002; the prize for

Best Educational Cartoon from the U<small>NICEF</small> Jury in 2005; and the Golden Prize at the Lifelong Learning Awards in Berlin, 2007. Publicized and well-known by its project name, the model has been developed in five languages—Italian, English, German, French and Spanish—for five years of language teaching (for each language) in nurseries and elementary schools. Teachers, educators and various specialists in inclusive and special needs education, as well as motivated non-specialists and parents from all over the world, have already applied the model successfully in their work and at home. Training courses for adults are offered in several European countries (see the *Hocus and Lotus* website).

The main activity of the lesson or "format" in *The Adventures of Hocus and Lotus* is a unique theatrical performance—a bouquet of words, actions and gestures. Adults and children enter a magic world of fantasy in the new language and take part in the stories of Hocus and Lotus and their friends. In the circle, all participants are involved at all times and relive the adventures of the little dinocrocs (half-dinosaurs, half-crocodiles), with whom it is easy for children to identify. The narratives are based on events from children's everyday lives and are deeply emotionally charged. They are full of surprises, twists and challenges. Children meet friends, play games, make mischief from time to time and even perform acts of bravery. They feel tired when they run and cold when they are in the rain, they feel happy with a friend around and sad when their friend leaves to go home. They solve problems and find solutions in different situations. Each format ends with a mini-musical, in which the children dance, move and sing, there is a cartoon to watch and a Dino book to read and write in. The cartoons, created for each "story of adventure" in collaboration with Italian TV (Rai Fiction), are broadcast in Bulgaria and in many other European countries as an educational cartoon series for children. Designed to glue children to the screen, they complement comprehension with visual clues and ensure consolidation of language acquisition by exposure to native speakers' pronunciation. What surfaces with practice and in time is a natural fluency in the new language.

The teachers are armed with a "magic kit" which offers all the necessary strategies for successful implementation of the model. The handbook contains the stories in five different languages. It is a detailed guide to the actions, gestures, facial expressions, gaze direction, voice intonation, *etc.*, used in the acting out of the stories. The self-training DVD included in the kit is an audio-visual version which enables the teachers to practice the acting of the episodes by watching and following the experts' acting recorded on the training video. So—all that is still needed is to choose a language to learn or teach and practice!

I DELIGHT IN the noise of the nursery and the beaming faces of the children and my students. I can't help wondering who is more enthusiastic—the little ones, or my wonderful, grown-up Sofia University dinocrocs?

References

Hocus and Lotus, the Little Dinocrocs that Teach Languages to Children. Website, <http://www.eng.hocus-lotus.edu/template.php?pag=70953>

Taeschner, Traute. *The Magic Teacher: Learning a Foreign Language at Nursery School—Results from the Project.* London: CILT Publications, 2005.

----------. *The Magic Teacher's Kit.* Rome: Dinocroc International Training Institute srl., 2004.

Tella, Seppo / Mononen-Aaltonen, Marja. "Developing Dialogic Communication Culture in Media Education: Integrating Dialogism and Technology." In: *Media Education Publication*, 7. Helsinki: University of Helsinki, 1998.

Zientek, Linda R. "Preparing High-Quality Teachers: Views from the Classroom." In: *American Educational Research Journal*, 44, 2007, 959-1001.

NOTE: This article was inspired by my work on the model with students of the Faculty of Pre-School and Primary School Education at Sofia University and the children at the 29th Nursery School "Slanze" ("The Sun"), whom we all dearly love. It is also linked with my work on a doctoral thesis in "Psicologia dell'orientamento e dei processi di apprendimento" ("Psychology of Career Guidance and Learning Strategies") at the University of Rome ("La Sapienza"). My supervisor Professor Taeschner, as well as my colleagues in Bulgaria, Professors Angelov, Danova and Shopov, and all the staff at the Department of Pre-School Education, were generous in helping me introduce the model at university level, so that we could take both students and children across the magic language bridge.

REDUCING OTHERNESS

by KLAUS SCHUBERT

MY SWEDISH UNCLE used to tell a story about a Swedish man and his British wife. When after a long marriage they decided to get divorced, the husband sighed: "This is what my mother always told me: It is risky to marry a foreigner." His wife replied: "*You* didn't marry a foreigner—*I* did!"

The conclusion seems to be that Otherness is always the Other's fault. In this short essay I shall address the issue of linguistic Otherness, and an attempt at reducing it. (And from here until my final paragraph I shall refrain from capitalizing the "o"—because this is not just a problem of profound philosophical significance, it is simultaneously a tricky question of practical everyday communication.)

What can you do when you encounter an *other*? In particular, when that other speaks another language? In principle, there are three options. We can speak my language. We can speak the other's language. Or we can speak a third language.

If we speak my language, I am in a superior position. I can phrase my points more fluently and more convincingly. I can take turns more quickly and thus be ahead of you. And, since the language is no problem, I can concentrate more time and effort on the subject that we are talking about rather than on how to express it. When a job is advertized for a person speaking my language, I shall probably get the job, and not the other, for whom my language is another language. On the other hand, when we speak my language and I fully exploit my pole position, it may well be that my brilliant rhetoric and sophisticated literary allusions are completely lost on my interlocutor. I may therefore be in a position of advantage with regard to expressing myself, but where do I stand with regard to being understood?

If we speak your language, I am in the inferior position. By the time I have construed a sentence and am about to start speaking, you have already said your piece and swung the argument in your direction. When I try to make a joke, you correct me and tell me that this is not the way things are put in your language.

Let us therefore look for other options. I could simply keep on speaking my language and you yours. If our languages are as close as, say, Swedish and Norwegian, this could work well. If our languages are distant and yet we keep on trying to communicate as best we can, we may in the long run give rise to a so-called *pidgin* language. This new language, when learnt by our children as their native tongue, can eventually turn into a *creole*. This option essentially means that because of the otherness of the others we create another language in which the otherness is removed. Or do we? We do not in a literal sense *create* a pidgin. It is something that emerges out of our common efforts to make ourselves understood to one another.

Yet another option would be to speak a third language taken from someone else. We should then both find ourselves in an inferior position, not so much *vis-à-vis* one another, but certainly in relation to the third party, the speakers of that vehicular language. And—to return to my uncle's anecdote—it could be really troublesome if you had, when speaking to your Swedish husband, to keep on reminding yourself how the *French* would put it.

So the idea of creating a completely new language is perhaps not so stupid after all. Wouldn't it be more straightforward, more effective and, for that matter, more fun? Deliberately creating a new language, a language which is neither mine, nor yours, nor theirs? But which could become *ours*?

The idea of deliberately creating a new language may be

counted among the dreams of mankind. Throughout history, people have created languages, and many of them have been documented and are still known to us. But creating a language system is only half the exercise. Obviously such a language is not much use unless it actually works in real communication. The first planned language whose author not only worked out and published a dictionary and a grammar, but also succeeded in establishing a small community of speakers and writers, was **Volapük**. It was created by Johann Martin Schleyer. His first publication appeared in 1879 in Sigmaringen, in the south-west of Germany, in a parish newsletter of restricted and local circulation. After some initial success, however, Schleyer published a book (1880), which is still available today in academic libraries.

Languages such as Volapük, deliberately created for international or interethnic communication, are called *planned languages*. The specialized discipline that devotes itself to their study is known as *interlinguistics*. Duličenko (1990) has compiled a catalog of known and documented planned language systems from antiquity until approximately the year 1973 which lists 912 languages. It goes without saying that some of the entries may be disputed, while on the other hand there must be many systems which were made known in such limited circles that they did not come to Duličenko's attention. But his industrious survey nevertheless gives an idea of the amount of work that has been invested in the project of deliberately creating a language other than mine and yours.

To arrange this multitude of languages in a clear and sensible order, the interlinguists use two main classificatory approaches. The first looks at the origin of the linguistic material, that is, the lexicon and the grammar. Moch (1897) is believed to have been the first to apply to the linguistic material of planned languages the criterion of the degree of artificiality *vs.* naturalness, or in other words the degree of inventedness *vs.* borrowedness (see Blanke 1985, 100; Sakaguchi 1998, 97). Moch labels languages with invented material *a priori* languages and those with material adopted from existing ethnic languages *a posteriori*.

The group of *a priori* languages is small. It includes mainly the languages sketched by philosophers like Descartes or Leibniz, often not primarily as a means of communication but as an instrument, or, in the language of our time, a representation, of heuristic and logical reasoning.

The group of *a posteriori* languages, by contrast, is large and varied. Interlinguists have complemented Moch's classification by further subdividing the *a posteriori* group by the same criterion of inventedness *vs.* borrowedness, labelling those languages with more invented words and grammatical rules *schematic* and those with a larger amount of borrowed elements *naturalist* languages. Examples of the schematic subgroup are **Esperanto** by Zamenhof (1887) and **Ido**, a reformed version of Esperanto, believed to have been devised by Couturat and de Beaufront (see Blanke 1985, 187). The naturalist subgroup includes languages such as **Occidental** by von Wahl (Blanke 1985, 161-67; Duličenko 219 f.), **Novial** by Jespersen (1928) and **Interlingua** by Gode (Gode / Blair 1951). This latter type has been described as systems imitating a group of languages, most often the Romance family.

Which of all these planned languages should we choose for our conversation with one another? The *a priori* languages can immediately be ruled out. They were not made for being learnt and they actually run counter to any mnemotechnique, so that they have to be considered unlearnable. So let us choose from the broad spectrum of *a posteriori* planned languages. What could be the criteria for this choice? We should choose the best language, of course! But what are the features of a language system that mark it out as being better than others? Is it the language that is easiest to learn? Or the one that is easiest to understand? The language that is easiest to learn is my native language, at least for me, and the language which you can most easily understand is yours, so this is not the right approach.

Let us therefore look not for superlatives but for an optimum—something which is not at the very top of one particular scale, but which is reasonably high up on many perhaps contradictory scales. We would thus be looking for the language that is easiest for me to learn while at the same time easiest for you to understand. This is likely to become complicated. Could we not simply take the most successful planned language? If something is successful, others must already have tried it out and found it useful.

This brings us to the other classification of planned languages commonly applied in interlinguistics. It was suggested by Blanke (1985, 107 f. and Table 2). While Moch looked at the origin of the linguistic material, Blanke analyzed how and for what purposes the language was being used. If Moch's approach is etymological, Blanke's is sociolinguistic. Moch analysed the *langue*, Blanke the *parole*. To rank the communicative situations and settings in which the language was used, Blanke established a scale of 28 steps (Blanke 2001). Its initial steps are (1) manuscript, (2) publication and (3) textbooks and learning materials, and the list continues until it reaches (26) family language, (27) element of an original culture and (28) language development.

Applying the criterion of communicative realization and assessing it by means of this scale, Blanke concludes that of the thousand or so known planned languages the vast majority have not progressed very far on the scale, a handful have attained some of the middle steps, and only a single one has reached the top of the ladder. The first group Blanke calls "projects", the middle group "semi-languages" and only the top tier is in Blanke's analysis assigned the label of a "planned language" proper. Volapük is found in the semi-language group, as are **Latino sine flexione** by Peano (1903), Ido, Occidental, Interlingua, and **Basic English** by Ogden (1930). It is interesting to find Basic English among the planned languages. Like Latino sine flexione, Basic English is a simplified variant of a single ethnic language, rather than being thoroughly composed of elements from several sources, as the typical *a posteriori* languages are. As such, Basic English is a forerunner of the controlled languages, such as are used in modern-day technical communication in industrial settings (Schubert 2001).

To return to Blanke's sociolinguistic classification of planned languages, the one and so far only representative of the group of communicatively fully realized languages, the planned languages proper, is Esperanto. This is why Arntz (2005, 333) has called Esperanto the most successful planned language by far.

We are still in search of a language which is neither mine nor yours, but is some optimum in between. A language less other than the other's. So far, we have encountered two planned languages which appear to be promising in this respect. These are Volapük and Esperanto. Volapük was the first communicatively realized planned language. It must therefore have some qualities which distinguish it from among all the other systems suggested previously. The other candidate is Esperanto. As the most successful planned language, it must somehow outdo all the others.

The design principles of Volapük follow the idea of meeting the other by making it easy for those who wish to learn the language. The lexicon is derived from English in the first place, German and French in the second and Spanish and Italian in the third (Schleyer 1880, 7). Schleyer devised twelve basic rules by means of which the words could be altered to fit into the system of Volapük (Schleyer 1888, x-xi). Some of these rules seem to be based simply on a personal preference of Schleyer's, such as when letters already used very often are left out. Other rules are obvious means of optimization also followed by other authors of planned (and controlled) languages, such as avoiding homonyms. But some appear to have been inspired by consideration of the other, for example replacing the sound [r] by [l] in many words to make life easier for the Chinese. Since all words are spelled phonemically and many words are shortened as compared to their origins, we then get words like *nol* ("knowledge"), *vol* ("world"), and *pük* ("speak"). Some of the words nicely reflect the pronunciation of English as it was taught in nineteenth-century Germany: *dök* ("duck"), or *löf* ("love").

Blanke (1985, 204-18) gives a thorough critical analysis of Volapük, its design principles and their realization, in which he points out that through all these alterations and, in addition, through an elaborate system of prefixes and suffixes the loaned words are altered to such an extent that they lose all mnemotechnical features. One should not, however, assume that planned languages can be devised so that they can be understood without learning on the basis of a command of the source language. Languages designed to function as a common denominator within a language family only, such as the pan-Romance or pan-Slavic languages, may follow this principle of immediate intelligibility, but it will not be achievable if a world-wide spread of the language is what is being aimed at. In the case of Volapük, however, the invented elements make up such a large a share of the language system that Volapük is classified as being of a mixed type between *a priori* and *a posteriori* (204).

Yet, Volapük was communicatively realized. It has functioned, and for some time it was very successful. The reasons for its rapid decline cannot be sought in the system alone. There must be additional, and as it appears, decisive reasons for its declining use as well. One of the most obvious phenomena in the development of Volapük and its community was Schleyer's inclination to hold on to authority over his language. He and he alone had the right to make changes in the lexicon or the grammar.

This is the point to turn to Esperanto. L. L. Zamenhof had no wish to be called the author or the master of his language. All he wanted was to be known as its *initiator*. When Volapük saw the light of day, Zamenhof was twenty and already laboring on his own language project, after his father had burned an earlier draft. Zamenhof had no money to publish a book, and so he took his time and developed the language in his study year after year, translating classical texts, writing original prose and composing poems. When, after this protracted "prototype phase", Zamenhof eventually spent his bride's dowry on the printing expenses and published a thin brochure under the pseudonym of "Dr. Esperanto" (Zamenhof 1887), he had already had ample time for trying out and thoroughly testing his language.

Esperanto is an *a posteriori* language. Its lexicon draws on Romance, Germanic and, to a lesser extent, Slavic stock. Its structure was apparently familiar to educated Europeans of the nineteenth century, but underneath the surface there was a radically novel system of meaning-bearing entities, what in modern linguistic terminology we would call completely agglutinative, extremely productive word formation with unchangeable morphemes (Schubert 1993). Nor does Esperanto pursue the idea of immediate intelligibility. Esperanto meets the other not by promoting comprehension without learning, but by enabling the other to speak and write in a highly regular system. It gives priority to active rather than passive easiness.

Zamenhof did not decline the title of author out of pure modesty. He had learned the lesson of Volapük, and so in the preface of this very first brochure Zamenhof resigned all rights to the language and placed his work in the hands of the language community. Despite this humble but far-sighted attitude, Zamenhof received a flood of letters from all over the growing language community with requests for advice on grammar, correctness, style and language use in general. Many of his conscientiously written answers have been lost, but fortunately a significant number were reprinted in the many journals and newsletters of the young language movement and a selection of these later collected in a book (Zamenhof 1927). Zamenhof gave many detailed answers, but in quite a few cases he refused. Instead of settling the issues submitted to him, Zamenhof time and again answered that several solutions were correct from a logical point of view and that the decision which one would be good Esperanto was not for him to make, but for those who used the language.

Zamenhof earned for Esperanto the title of the most successful planned language not by telling others how to use it, nor by steering and constraining it, but by devising a system with the capacity to develop and then letting it do so.

This may be all very well, but of course outside observers often confidently judge declare that this entire planned language stuff is no good, since an artificially made language cannot carry a culture and will never replace our native languages. Neither mine, nor the other's. And that, no matter how far up Esperanto has climbed on Blanke's scale. These wholesale rejections of planned languages are difficult to argue with, since they normally lack any empirical underpinning, let alone knowledge of the object of study. But what about the view of a renowned linguist like Louis Hjelmslev? In his analysis, an artificial symbol system cannot achieve the expressive power of a natural language. Or, as Hjelmslev puts it, an artificial symbol system can be translated into a natural language, but not the other way round (Hjelmslev 1943, 97). Blanke's analysis, in stating that Esperanto is an element of an original culture (Blanke's step 27), would seem to contradict this. Who is right? In my opinion, both are. The solution lies in the 26 steps to be passed prior to the cultural stage. In other words, I think that Hjelmslev's diagnosis is correct and that it accurately describes the expressive power of Esperanto—as it was in 1887. Since then, however, people have started using the language. They speak and write to one another in Esperanto. At first, they must have had to make do with the limited expressiveness of a newly devised, artificial system. But, step by step, the use of Esperanto expanded, the communicative situations became more and more varied, norms developed and a language community came into being, albeit a second-language community.

When the Other is encountered in a fully developed planned language, the Self and the Other meet on common ground. When I write this article in English, some friendly editor has to spend hours transposing it into something which meets the norms of the English language community [Theoretically, yes, but in this case it wasn't too arduous!—*Ed.*]. Learning English did not and will not make me a member of that community. A planned language, however, has a second-language community. As soon as I acquire a reasonable command of it, I am a member of that community. My language use will contribute to the norms of the community. The Other will join the same community. Here is a means to reduce Otherness.

References

Arntz, Reiner. "Sprachplanung und Plansprachen—auch ein Thema für die Übersetzerausbildung." In: *Kultur, Interpretation, Translation*. Ed. Heidemarie Salevsky. Frankfurt/M.: Lang, 2005, 329-41.

Blanke, Detlev. *Internationale Plansprachen. Eine Einführung (Sammlung Akademie-Verlag Sprache, 34)*. Berlin: Akademie-Verlag, 1985.

------------. "Vom Entwurf zur Sprache" (2001). Revised version. In: Detlev Blanke. *Interlinguistische Beiträge*. Ed. Sabine Fiedler. Frankfurt/M.: Lang, 2006, 49-98, 339-90.

Duličenko, Aleksandr Dmitrievič. *Meždunarodnye vspomogatel'nye jazyki*. Tallinn: Valgus, 1990.

Gode, Alexander / Blair, Hugh E. *Interlingua: A Grammar of the International Language* (1951). Second edition, second printing. New York: Ungar, 1971.

Hjelmslev, Louis. *Omkring sprogteoriens grundlæggelse* (1943). Second edition. Copenhagen: Akademisk Forlag, 1966.

Jespersen, Otto. *An international language*. London: George Allen & Unwin, 1928.

Moch, Gaston. *La question de la langue internationale et sa solution par l'Espéranto*. Paris: Giard & Brière, 1897.

Ogden, Charles K. *Basic English*. London: Trübner, 1930.

Peano, Giuseppe. "De Latino sine flexione." In: *Rivista di matematica*, 8, 3, 1903, 74-83.

Sakaguchi, Alicja. *Interlinguistik: Gegenstand, Ziele, Aufgaben, Methoden*. Frankfurt/M.: Lang, 1998.

Schleyer, Johann Martin. *Volapük: Die Weltsprache—Entwurf einer Universalsprache für alle Gebildete der ganzen Erde* (1880). Reprint, edited by Reinhard Haupenthal.

Hildesheim: Olms, 1982.

------------. *Grosses Wörterbuch der Universalsprache Volapük*. Fourth edition. Constance: Schleyer, 1888.

Schubert, Klaus. "Semantic Compositionality." In: *Linguistics*, 31, 1993, 311-65.

------------. "Gestaltete Sprache: Plansprachen und die regulierten Sprachen der internationalen Fachkommunikation." In: *Planned Languages: From Concept to Reality*. Ed. Klaus Schubert. Brussels: Hogeschool voor Wetenschap en Kunst, 2001, 223-57.

Zamenhof, L. L. [under the pseudonym "Dr. Ėsperanto"]. *Meždunarodnyj jazyk*. Warsaw: Kel'ter, 1887. Also as website, <http://anno.onb.ac.at/cgi-content/anno-buch?apm=0&aid=100082&zoom=>

------------. *Lingvaj respondoj*. (1927). Posthumous publication, edited by Gaston Waringhien. Ninth edition. Marmande: Esperantaj Francaj Eldonoj, 1962.

ABOUT THE AUTHORS

Jesús Baigorri Jalón teaches interpreting at the University of Salamanca (Spain). A former United Nations staff interpreter, he has published several works on the history of interpreting and on intercultural communication. Dr. Baigorri is the director of the *Grupo Alfaqueque* research group and is a practicing interpreter.

Hansjörg Bittner is a lecturer in translation studies at the University of Hildesheim. He is of the opinion that language is not just a means to an end but an end in itself. As a literary man who won a British Academy Award to develop a metrical theory of free verse and then spent a year trying to make students in Cyprus understand it, Dr. Bittner particularly enjoys the challenges of translating English poetry into German. He is also a business English trainer and translator for companies in and around Hamburg.

Elke Bosse taught at universities in Germany, Brazil and Turkey before joining the Institute of Intercultural Communication at the University of Hildesheim. Interested in both theory and practice, Dr. Bosse has, on the one hand, completed extensive research into intercultural training, while also coordinating a project to promote intercultural learning as an essential part of the internationalization of universities. She was the recipient of an excellence in teaching award for 2009-10.

Marit Breede works in the International Office of the University of Hildesheim. She wrote her doctoral thesis on intercultural encounters in alternative tourism. When she is not in the office, you'll probably find her in the woods, birdwatching or running.

Madeleine Danova is professor of North American literature and culture in the department of English and American Studies at the University of Sofia (Bulgaria). She has been involved in several international projects on ethnicity, nationalism, language and identity. Her most recent book (English text) is *Transformations of the Ethnic Occult in Twentieth-century North American Literature: Hybrid Identities and Diasporic Glocalities at the Borders* (forthcoming from Sofia University Press). Dr. Danova has been on the board of several professional organizations, and is editor-in-chief of the literary journal *Vox Litterarum*.

Helena Drawert studied at universities in Germany and Spain, and is now teaching and researching linguistics and intercultural communication at the University of Hildesheim. One day she is going to sail around the world.

Joachim Griesbaum is professor of information science at the University of Hildesheim. The main focus of his teaching and research is on social media. Dr. Griesbaum is fond of tigers and diving, but (like most people) would prefer not to actually encounter any fierce creatures in the wild.

Ioulia Grigorieva is a research assistant in the Institute of Intercultural Communication at the University of Hildesheim, researching for a doctorate in Russian-German communication. Apart from Russian, she is also passionately interested in beach volleyball (without jump serves), literature, and music beyond the mainstream.

Francis Jarman teaches comparative cultural studies and intercultural communication at the University of Hildesheim. According to family tradition, he is descended from the Thracian slave Androcles (of "Androcles and the Lion" fame). In 2009, Dr. Jarman was awarded the Erasmus Prize of the German Academic Exchange Service. He is also a playwright, novelist and classical numismatist.

Berenike Kuschel worked as a research assistant in the Institute of Intercultural Communication at the University of Hildesheim before leaving to teach at Tongji University (Shanghai, China), another university with a highly intercultural profile. She was the recipient of a Hildesheim excellence in teaching award for 2009-10.

Anne-Kristin Langner is a doctoral student in the Institute of Media and Theater, University of Hildesheim, researching into television phenomena in an intercultural context. In 2006, she was awarded a Certificate of Achievement for outstanding academic performance by the University of Nicosia, Cyprus. She also works as a journalist, writes short stories, and takes a strong interest in Swedish language and culture.

Thomas Mandl is professor of information science at the University of Hildesheim. His research interests include information retrieval, human-computer interaction and internationalization of information technology, and he has published on multilingual information systems and quality of web pages. Dr. Mandl is the descendant of a Croatian bodyguard of the famous "Sissi" (Empress Elisabeth of Austria), and is a well-known figure on the German beach volleyball scene.

Detelina Metz is professor of text linguistics in the department of German and Scandinavian Studies at the University of Sofia (Bulgaria). She has been involved in a number of international projects on migration and multilingualism, creative writing, and mass media studies. Dr. Metz has published extensively on the language of the media, TV advertisements, the color code in language, and sociolinguistics. She and her husband, a German banker, live on the outskirts of Sofia.

Maria Möstl finished her MA degree in international information management at the University of Hildesheim in 2010 with a thesis on self-expression in online social networks. She is currently working at an online marketing agency in Hamburg.

Concepción Otero Moreno teaches translation and interpreting at the University of Hildesheim. Dr. Otero is a member of the *Grupo Alfaqueque* research group and has published several works on methodology for teaching translation and interpreting. She is a court interpreter.

Manju Ramanan or "Mango Romanian" according to spell check has no connections with Romania. An Indian journalist with ten years' experience and an MPhil in post-colonial Canadian writing, she is currently working with Sterling Publications in Dubai Media City. She does like mangoes, however.

Klaus Schubert is professor of applied linguistics and international specialized communication at the University of Hildesheim. Dr. Schubert owes his career to the language most prominently described in his article.

Vasco da Silva studied languages and business adminstration in Germany and Spain, and is currently teaching and researching in intercultural communication at the University of Hildesheim. Due to his partly Portuguese roots he is deeply interested in the cultures of the Iberian peninsula, and he is a great fan of contemporary Spanish art.

Ekaterina Sofronieva teaches linguistics at Sofia University (Bulgaria) and is doing research in psychology at the University of Rome "La Sapienza". As she grows older and wiser, she takes a deeper interest in issues of empathy, love and compassion that go beyond language boundaries. Her friends tell her that she should seriously commit to writing, since the poems and stories she wrote when she was six are better than the ones that she writes now.

Christa Womser-Hacker is professor of information science at the University of Hildesheim. Dr. Womser-Hacker's main research interests are in multilingual information retrieval, intercultural human-computer interaction and evaluation, and she is very much attracted by numbers and measurements.